THY KINGDOM COME
THE VISION

By Keith Rodriguez, Nelson Warner, and Tom Pears

K2 Series, Book 2 of 4

ISBN-13:978-1547168361
ISBN-10:1547168366
First Printing: July, 2017
Cover design by Ray Ogle
Cover photo by Kelly Morvant at Oak Alley Plantation, Vacherie, LA
Printed in the United States

The *K2 Series* is a God-inspired and God-led collaboration among Keith Rodriguez, Nelson Warner, and Tom Pears. K2 stands for and symbolizes the King & the Kingdom. The *K2 Series* is the brand name given to the ongoing series of books and future products created to communicate God's Purpose for those who love Him—conforming us to the image and character of Jesus Christ. This purpose is the silver thread that harmonizes the *K2 Series*. The four titles with subtitles and book numbers are:

- *K2 Series: Our Father in Heaven: The Motivation* (Book One)
- *K2 Series: Thy Kingdom Come: The Vision* (Book Two)
- *K2 Series: Thy Will Be Done: The Mission* (Book Three)
- *K2 Series: On Earth as it is in Heaven: The Application* (Book Four)

ACKNOWLEDGMENTS

The authors want to thank Ray Ogle for his creative insights, technical experience, encouragement, cover design, and faithful friendship over the years of developing the *K2 Series*. The authors want to thank our editors, Carol Stubbs and Nancy Rust with Copper Iris Books, for their experience, editing, and formatting expertise. We especially thank Ray and our editors for their patience and perseverance. We offer a special thank you to Suzette Morvant Magee for transcribing a few of our *K2* class audios. We thank the participants of our four different K2 Study Groups who helped us better develop this four book *K2 Series* over the past five years. The authors also want to thank our many mentors and teachers whose shoulders we stand on and whose footsteps we walk in as we all follow Christ. And of course our greatest gratitude goes to Jesus Christ, our Savior and Lord.

Thy kingdom come...
(Matthew 6:10a, KJV)

THY KINGDOM COME
The Vision

But first and most importantly seek (aim at, strive after) His kingdom and His righteousness [His way of doing and being right—the attitude and character of God], and all these things will be given to you also.
(Matthew 6:33, AMP)

CONTENTS

INTRODUCTION

The Eagle and Turkey Parable

Once upon a time there was an eagle's egg that fell from its nest high in a tree. It landed unharmed in a soft bed of leaves and rolled down the hill.

In the valley far below, a flock of foraging turkeys found the unbroken egg. One of the mother turkeys brought the eagle egg back to her nest. The young eaglet soon hatched and first saw the mother turkey that "imprinted" her identity on the eaglet. The eaglet began life thinking and knowing itself as a turkey.

The whole flock of turkeys made constant fun of the eaglet, telling him that he was the ugliest turkey ever. They laughed at his big feet and his screechy gobble. The young eaglet felt incomplete and sad. Even though down deep in his soul he knew something was not right, the eaglet believed he was who the turkeys told him he was.

One day while the flock was out foraging on the ground for bugs and seeds, Father Eagle above saw the turkey flock, and there in their midst was his lost son. As Father Eagle watched, he realized that his son acted like a turkey! "My son believes that he is a turkey!"

The eaglet had unknowingly allowed the mother turkey and flock of turkeys to imprint their image on him. He had conformed to their image and likeness. He sadly knew no differently and saw no other way. He did not know who he was or that he was created to be like his father.

As Father Eagle watched, his heart burned within for his son to know the truth of who he was truly created to be. He had to tell his son the truth! Father Eagle immediately flew down to tell his son, but the turkeys and his son all scattered in fear as his shadow covered them. The eaglet was afraid of his own father's shadow!

Father Eagle ultimately understood that he must somehow go live among the turkeys until they could trust him and his son could hear him. To live like the turkeys, he would have to stay on the ground and not fly anymore like eagles do. Over time he slowly became like a turkey to the turkeys, and the flock slowly began to accept him. Building this trust took a very long time, but finally Father Eagle was able to pick bugs and seeds right alongside the turkeys without frightening them.

While alongside them, Father Eagle was able to come close to his son. The father began whispering to the eaglet, "I love you. You are not who you think you are or who they say you are."

Father Eagle began telling the eaglet about flying and effortlessly soaring high over mountains and seas on rising currents of air, but the eaglet was scared. He told his father that he was afraid of heights and that turkeys don't fly very well or very far. He, like all turkeys, liked the ground and felt comfortable there. "Furthermore," the son asked, "how can a turkey eat if not on the ground?" The eaglet son was very fearful and skeptical of what his father was trying to tell him. He clung tightly to his imprinted image of being a turkey and refused to let go.

One day as the eaglet was drinking water at the pond, Father Eagle came alongside him. In the pond's reflecting surface, and side by side with his father, he for the first time saw his likeness in his father. That was a huge "aha" moment for the eaglet! He might not be who the turkeys told him he was, or even who he thought he was. The eaglet soon began watching the bigger eagle more and more. The deep sadness he held in his heart began giving way to something good, true, and beautiful. There was a stirring deep in the eaglet's soul. There was a largeness in Father Eagle that went far beyond his physical size. There was something very exciting happening within the eaglet for the first time ever, especially when Father Eagle stood close by and lovingly said to the eaglet, "Follow Me...Do not be afraid, I will be with you always...You are much more than you think you are...I love and admire you, my son." Finally, the eaglet let go of the fear and pain of being a turkey and excitedly embraced the joy of becoming an eagle. He let go of "turkey-ism" and followed his father's way to being who he was created in his father's image to become.

Eagle teaching and training began in earnest. In much grace and truth, Father Eagle began gently encouraging the eaglet,

"Follow me, son, and you will see who you truly are and created to be."

Following his father, the eaglet began to experience a transformation that is akin to becoming a new creation. Father Eagle began teaching and training the eaglet in the way of eagles. As the eaglet learned, he began to discover little by little and more and more his true identity, meaning, and purpose in life.

After much following, teaching, and training the eaglet began spreading his beautiful wings and feeling the freedom and power. The turkey in him began to die, and the eagle in him began to live. He soared high above the trees with Father Eagle, and other eagles joined them. The eaglet found completeness and joy in being himself and united in the larger brotherhood and family of eagles. It was a long fearful road allowing the turkey image in him to die, but when he did, he truly discovered a life of wholeness that his soul so deeply longed for—a life of freedom and power that allowed him to love and to be loved in his true family, a soaring life full of joy that allowed him to see and experience who he truly was. He had the life that he was originally created to be—in the image and likeness of his father. The eagle now knew in his heart that he was in his father and his father was in him.

Note:

There is a phenomenon in nature known as "imprinting." Scientific studies on this phenomenon were first done in the early 1900's. An Austrian naturalist, Konrad Lorenz, became the first to codify and establish the science behind the imprinting process. Lorenz found that when young birds came out of their eggs, they would become attached to the first moving object they encountered. In most cases in the wild, that would be their mother. But Lorenz replaced himself as the object of their affection. And it wasn't just he that the young birds would attach to as a mother substitute. They would just as easily attach to inanimate objects and oddities, such as a pair of gumboots, a white ball, and even an electric train–if it was presented at the right time. Birds and mammals are born with a pre-programmed drive to imprint. Lorenz's work with geese and ducks provided concrete evidence that there are critical sensitive periods in life where certain types of learning can take place. And, once that learning is "fixed," it is the least likely to be forgotten or unlearned. Lorenz's geese responded to him as a parent, following him about everywhere, and when they became adults, courted him in preference to other geese!

("My Life as a Turkey," published by PBS, *Nature*, November 12, 2012)

This eaglet is like us, who are created in the image and likeness of our Creator (Genesis 1:26). We are not who the "fallen" world tells us we are and not who we envision ourselves to be. We are much more. God desires mankind to know who we truly are. He tells us to first and foremost seek and aim at His Kingdom and His righteous character (Matthew 6:33) for a reason.

Nelson:

> One of my elderly mentors once asked, "Can you succinctly and biblically describe the Kingdom of God?" I spouted something off, but I truly did not know what to say. It was obvious that I had no biblical vision of the Kingdom of God on earth as it is in heaven. When we go from "here-to-there," it is most important to know where the "there" is and develop a biblical vision of the "there." As the saying goes, "If you do not know where you are going, you will end up someplace else." And then there is the parable of how the blind cannot lead the blind. We need to know where we are heading and, in the Will of God, allow God's Word and Spirit to lead us there. Jesus prayed, "Thy kingdom come, Thy will be done on earth, as it is in heaven" (Matthew 6:10, KJV).

Matthew 6:10 indicates our destination is the Kingdom of God, while pointing out the pathway to the Kingdom as the Will of God. *Thy Kingdom Come,* will biblically develop a kingdom vision, while the next *K2* book in the series, *Thy Will Be Done,* will biblically develop God's mission for us.

Remember that God's original intention for mankind is the Garden of Eden, the Kingdom of God. Let us first, and most importantly, aim at the vision of both the King's Kingdom and His character.

> But first and most importantly seek (aim at, strive after) His kingdom and His righteousness [His

way of doing and being right—the attitude and character of God], and all these things will be given to you also."
(Matthew 6:33, AMP)

In this book, *Thy Kingdom Come*, we will be asking the Word of God to reveal the character of the Kingdom, while also asking Scripture what the character of our King is. In studying our Lord's character, we also find that God has purposed us individually and as His family to conform to God's character. This process requires us to be released from our burden of sin (freedom) and then be developed and empowered to look like Christ Jesus in the Kingdom of God on earth.

As followers of Christ become a threat to Satan's kingdom, we come under attack. When this happens, we need to put on the Armor of God. This book will discuss how the character of God relates to the Armor of God. We learn that God is not just a God of Salvation, but also a God of development and empowerment for His Kingdom's sake.

Through New Covenant grace, we are released and empowered to willingly enter the spiritual battle. God the Father sent His Son, His Son sent His Spirit, and His Spirit now sends the Church for the King's Kingdom's sake and glory. Where are we sent? On earth as it is in heaven.

After our salvation moment, let's commit ourselves to embracing God's purpose of growing up in Christ-likeness. Let's conform to the vision of His image for the Kingdom's sake. Our Christian character develops along the pathway of agape love that empowers us. Our character and true self are developed through the struggle and pain of dying to our fallen and false self by choosing to love both God and others before self. As for our children, let's make sure they do not leave home without a clear vision of where they are going and the character to get there. Our children need to be freed and empowered to lovingly become God's light in this dark world. Being our children's shepherds, we should ask them to follow us, as we follow Christ Jesus. Let's give them the vision of a better tomorrow in the Kingdom of God on earth. In His hands we can rest assured.

In the next *K2* Book, *Thy Will be Done*, our mission will be examined.

CHAPTER ONE

The Character of God

Nelson:

In my exuberance after accepting Christ, I immediately asked people around me, "What's next?" They told me that I was to go convert others to Christianity. Soon thereafter, I was invited to join a disciple group studying the Navigator's *2.7 Series*, which began directing me toward creating good spiritual habits that ultimately taught me better ways of evangelizing non-believers. But no one could tell me where I was going, unless evangelism was the end goal! While evangelism is a good thing, it seemed like there was nothing beyond the salvation moment except the eternal. There seemed to be no vision in the here and now. In my past business and sports life, I had always aimed at a vision, a goal. That is, I would always begin with the end in mind. Beginning with the end in mind speaks to having a vision, a destination, a goal. Beginning with the end in mind requires us to know where we are going. As in using a road map, it is important to have a destination in mind, so we don't get off track or waste our time with things that divert our attention and energy. While the "there" is important, it is also vital to know where the "here" is too. Once we know our location and our destination, a plan can be mapped out to get us from here to there. My "here" was located just inside the door of my conversion, salvation, or justification moment. But what was God's purpose for me after my moment of justification? I finally began learning that after conversion God's purpose for me and all of His followers is to be conformed to the image of His Son. The ultimate 'there' is possessing Christ-like character in the Kingdom family on earth as it is in heaven. After our salvation or justification moment, our "here-to-there" journey is called the sanctification process of growing up and maturing in Christ-likeness. In desiring to begin with the end in mind, I needed to develop a biblical, Christ-like vision of who I was to become. So in an effort to develop God's vision for me and His Body, I prayerfully went to Scripture with the question, "How does the Bible succinctly describe the character of God?"

As we study the Word of God, we can begin to discern God's purpose for the lives of those who have chosen to trust and love Jesus Christ and His Word. This process or idea of accepting Jesus in order to be saved is sometimes seen as a single step followed by a time of rest because salvation is assured. But, this is only a first step; God has much more in mind for Christ-followers. On the one hand, He wants us to see Jesus as the author and guarantor of the covenant to bring so many of us into relationship with Him. Jesus is the King and we are His subjects, but He treats us as so much more. Jesus calls us His friends, and He has even more in store for us. This can be seen best in Romans 8:28 (NASB), "And we know that God causes all things to work together for good to those who love God, to those who are called according to His purpose."

You might ask, "What is that purpose?" Do you know your purpose? Look at the next verse, "For whom He foreknew, He also predestined to become conformed to the image of His Son, so that He would be the first-born among many brethren." Then Paul goes on to tell us that those He predestined, He called. And those He called, He justified and those He justified, He gave them His glory. What a progression! Clearly, the justification and salvation moment is not His only goal for us. For whatever time we spend on this planet, God wants each of us to grow to look more and more like His Son, as He develops His glorious character in us. As the Scripture says, this development is the purpose for which we are predestined. And God will graciously do it all (Romans 8:32). Later in Romans 12:2 (NIV) Paul writes, "Do not conform to the pattern of this world, but be transformed by the renewing of your mind. Then you will be able to test and approve what God's will is—his good, pleasing and perfect will."

Brennan Manning, in his book *Ruthless Trust,* tells us, "It must be noted that Jesus reveals who God is. He is the source of our information about transcendence/divinity. We cannot deduce anything about Jesus from what we think we know about God; however, we must deduce everything about God from what we know about Jesus." In John 14:7-9, Jesus said, "If you know Me you know the Father. If you have seen me you have seen the Father."

Paul tells us in Colossians 1:15a (NASB), "He [Jesus] is the image of the invisible God." The character of Jesus reflects the character of God. And when developed in us, these character traits conform us to Jesus' likeness. In that way, the Kingdom of God can appear on earth in "many brethren" and the invisible becomes visible.

God's sanctifying-glorifying process is slow. Many times, when wondering if we are being conformed to His image and character, we must look back and remember who we once were. In looking back, can we see our transformation? We also must have in mind a vision of who we are becoming. That is, what is the character of God, and what does He purpose us to become?

God is Sovereign: Supreme in Power and Authority

God is infinite, eternal, all present, all powerful, all-knowing, unchanging, wise, and holy. "Hallowed be Thy Name." God is sovereign over all creation. God is mystically beyond our understanding. Yet, Scripture gives a revelation of God's character in a way we can grasp and understand.

The Revealed Character of God:
A Psalms Study

So, what are God's revealed character traits that are to be developed in believers? Simply put, these traits reflect gracefulness, faithfulness, love, righteousness, justice, and shalom (wholeness, joy, peace). The remainder of this lesson will probe these revealed character traits of God as described in Psalms.

> Righteousness and Justice are the foundation of
> Your throne; love and faithfulness go before You.
> (Psalm 89:14, NIV)

> Love and faithfulness meet together;
>   righteousness and peace kiss each other.
> Faithfulness springs forth from the earth,
>   and righteousness looks down from heaven.
> The Lord will indeed give what is good,
>   and our land will yield its harvest.
> Righteousness goes before him
>   and prepares the way for his steps.
> (Psalm 85:10-13, NIV)

Oswald Chambers, in his daily devotional for September 1 in *My Utmost for His Highest*, asks "What is the purpose of your life?" Chambers then states, "The destined end of man is not happiness, but holiness."

As God designed us to become what we love most and value the highest, God's character and high ideals gradually become our Christ-like character too. So, beginning with the end in

5

mind, our goal then is to become more and more like Christ Jesus in our character. This process demands that we begin to explore and process how the Holy Scripture explicitly paints the character of God and His Holiness.

> Because it is written, "YOU SHALL BE HOLY, FOR I AM HOLY."
> (1 Peter 1:16, NASB)

Psalms writers repeatedly describe God's major character traits as being the following:

- Graceful,
- Faithful,
- Loving,
- Righteous,
- Just,
- Shalom (whole, peaceful, joyful).

Note: There are many biblical attributes for God, such as goodness, forgiveness, truthfulness, mercy, and compassion, which all basically fit under the six character traits listed above. The *K2 Series* is not attempting to place our sovereign God in a box, but is attempting to begin a dialogue and a struggle to understand and to grow up together in Christ-likeness as His Body. These six principal characteristics are the very things through which the holiness of God's Character is being developed in us who believe, who allow ourselves to be taught and actively guided by the Word of God and the Spirit of God in us. It is in our being conformed to His image that we glorify our Lord. We invite you to join our developmental struggle to rightly learn and to care and do as Christ Jesus does without causing further harm to ourselves and others. In the *K2 Series* we will discover how these six big character traits form a process of becoming like the King and Kingdom (on earth as it is in heaven).

Grace

We generally define grace as being God's unmerited favor. God created everything, including man and woman and "it was very good" (Genesis 1:31). God then graciously gave man and woman the stewardship of His Good Creation. Everything we have is a gift from God. Our breath itself is grace. Thus, all blessings graciously flow from our Lord and Creator. Grace is an all-inclusive word and concept. God's graciousness, while not explicitly mentioned in Psalms, is the underlying theme, and it is most deserving of our constant thankfulness and praise. Consider the underlining theme of grace in the following verses in Psalm 103:2-8, AMP:

> "Bless *and* affectionately praise the Lord, O my soul, And do not forget any of His benefits [grace]; Who forgives [grace] all your sins, Who heals [grace] all your diseases; Who redeems [grace] your life from the pit, Who crowns [grace] you [lavishly] with lovingkindness [grace] and tender mercy [grace]; Who satisfies [grace] your years with good things [grace], So that your youth is renewed [grace] like the [soaring] eagle. The Lord executes righteousness [grace] and justice [grace] for all the oppressed. He made known [grace] His ways [of righteousness and justice] [grace] to Moses, His acts [grace] to the children of Israel. The Lord is merciful [grace] and

gracious, Slow to anger [grace] and abounding in compassion [grace] *and* lovingkindness [grace].

Christ's New Covenant grace given to believers is purposed to both free and powerfully transform and conform us to the image of His noble character (Romans 8:28-29): gracefulness, faithfulness, love, righteousness, justice, and shalom.

While reading Psalms, consider how gracious our Lord is. Consider how His Grace and Shalom (wholeness, peacefulness, joyfulness) form the bookends to God's other character traits of being Faithful, Loving, Right, and Just. Meditate day and night on how these character traits are interrelated and interdependent with each other like a chain. Christ-like character is the image and likeness man was originally created to be and is now to become.

Read Psalms while meditating on the revealed Character of God. Over time you will see these same character traits repeat themselves throughout Scripture. Here are a few of the many verses in Psalms that describe the Character of God:

> If You, Lord, should mark iniquities, O Lord, who could stand? But there is forgiveness [grace] with You, That You may be feared.
> (Psalm 130:3-4, NKJV)

> He has made His wonderful works to be remembered; The Lord is gracious and full of compassion.
> (Psalm 111:4, NKJV)

Surely, LORD, you bless the righteous; you
surround them with your favor [grace]
as with a shield.
(Psalm 5:12, NIV)

The LORD is known by his acts of justice;
(Psalm 9:16a, NIV)

For the LORD is righteous, he loves justice; the
upright will see his face.
(Psalm 11:7, NIV)

For the word of the LORD is right and true; he is
faithful in all he does. The LORD loves
righteousness and justice; the earth is full of his
unfailing love.
(Psalm 33:4-5, NIV)

Your love, LORD, reaches to the heavens, your
faithfulness to the skies. Your righteousness is like
the highest mountains, your justice like the great
deep. You, LORD, preserve both people and
animals.
(Psalm 36:5-6, NIV)

 I do not hide your righteousness in my heart; I
speak of your faithfulness and your saving help. I do
not conceal your love and your faithfulness from
the great assembly. Do not withhold your mercy
from me, LORD; may your love and faithfulness
always protect me.
(Psalm 40:10-11, NIV)

And the heavens proclaim his righteousness, for he is a God of justice.
(Psalm 50:6, NIV)

Love and faithfulness meet together; righteousness and peace kiss each other. Faithfulness springs forth from the earth, and righteousness looks down from heaven.
(Psalm 85:10-11, NIV)

But you, Lord, are a compassionate and gracious God, slow to anger, abounding in love and faithfulness.
(Psalm 86:15, NIV)

I will sing of the LORD's great love forever; with my mouth I will make your faithfulness known through all generations. I will declare that your love stands firm forever, that you have established your faithfulness in heaven itself...Righteousness and justice are the foundation of your throne; love and faithfulness go before you...but I will not take My love from him, nor will I ever betray My faithfulness. I will not violate My covenant or alter what my lips have uttered.
(Psalm 89:1-2, 14, 33-34, NIV)

I will sing of your love and justice; to you, LORD, I will sing praise.
(Psalm 101:1, NIV)

...who redeems your life from the pit and crowns you with love and compassion...The LORD works

righteousness and justice for all the oppressed...The LORD is compassionate and gracious, slow to anger, abounding in love.
(Psalm 103:4, 6, 8; NIV)

For great is your love, higher than the heavens; your faithfulness reaches to the skies.
(Psalm 108:4, NIV)

The LORD is gracious and righteous; our God is full of compassion.
(Psalm 116:5, NIV)

God is Full of Grace

By the love shown to us on the Cross, we are saved by grace through faith and not by anything we did. Grace is the unmerited "gifts of God."

> For it is by grace you have been saved, through faith—and this is not from yourselves, it is the gift of God—not by works, so that no one can boast.
> (Ephesians 2:8-9, NIV)

So, not only can man not earn grace, man is unworthy and undeserving of God's saving grace. Yet God lovingly and freely offers grace to all people who willingly turn to Him and accept His gift by wholeheartedly trusting in Jesus Christ their Savior, Lord and God. By grace through faith in the truth of

11

Jesus Christ we are now forgiven, equipped, and blessed with every spiritual blessing.

Too often, we try to pigeonhole "grace" into an exclusive meaning, when in truth it is a broad, powerful, all-inclusive term. God's unmerited favor and gifts in Psalms are implicitly expressed in the following words: all blessings, wisdom, spirit, forgiveness, understanding, truth, salvation, power, inheritance, rest, light, life, creation, God's works/deeds/creation, joy, rest, law, word, decrees, statutes, guidance, favored, refuge, instructs, teaches, councils, hope, preserves, protects, rescues, fortress, frees, land, help, strength, incarnation, reconcile, redeem, kindness, mercy, favor, and compassion.

We use many synonyms for grace in our everyday language: favor, kindness, merciful favor, benevolence, benignity, blessing, clemency, compassion, forbearance, forgiveness, gentleness, kindness, lenience, leniency, lenity, mercy, mildness, pardon, pity, and tenderness.

We use many antonyms for grace in our everyday language: cruelty, hardness, harshness, implacability, penalty, punishment, revenge, rigor, severity, sternness, vengeance.

God is Faithful and True
He always does what He says He will do

Everyone has faith in something. The question is, "Faith in what?" Faith demands an object. Some people place their faith in the secular and temporal, while others place their faith in the spiritual and eternal. Secular faith is generally focused on an object that is seen, measured, and known, like money. A person who bases his or her faith in the secular and temporal must see-it-to-believe-it. Christian faith, on the other hand, reflects the unseen aspects of our spirit being awakened by God's Spirit and eternity. Faith must have an object. The object of Christian faith is anchored in the Truth of Jesus Christ and His promises. Faith and Truth are inseparable. Christian faith believes-to-see, not sees-to-believe.

> For we live by faith, not by sight.
> (2 Corinthians 5:7, NIV)

What is Faith?

> Now faith is the assurance (title deed, confirmation) of things hoped for (divinely guaranteed), and the evidence of things not seen [the conviction of their reality—faith comprehends as fact what cannot be experienced by the physical senses].
> (Hebrews 11:1, AMP)

Faith is explained as the confident assurance that what we hope for is going to happen. Faith starts with believing in God's character; that He is who He says He is. Faith culminates with believing in God's promises that He will do what He says He will do. For believers, "hope" is a desire based on assurance, and the assurance is based on God's character. Faith

is the evidence of things we cannot yet see, meaning that we have complete confidence that God will fulfill His promises, even though we don't yet see any evidence. These include eternal life, future rewards, heaven, and so forth. Faith regards these to be as real as what can be perceived with the senses. This conviction about God's unseen promises allows Christians to persevere in their faith regardless of persecution, opposition, and temptation.
(*Life Applications New Testament Commentary*, pages 1042-43)

God is faithful (reliable, trustworthy, and therefore ever true to His promise, and He can be depended on); by Him you were called into companionship and participation with His Son, Jesus Christ our Lord.
(1 Corinthians 1:9, AMP).

In Hebrew, *emeth* (*Strong's Concordance* #571) means firmness, faithfulness, truth. *Emeth* originates from the Hebrew word *aman*.

In Greek, *pistis* (*Strong's Concordance* #4102), means conviction of the truth of anything: belief; fidelity and faithfulness in the character of one who can be relied on.

God's faithfulness and truth flow out of His grace. The faithfulness and truthfulness of God's character is our most reliable place to make our stand, to walk, and to embrace His character.

Our Christian faith is modeled and anchored in the truth of Jesus Christ and includes biblical verbs such as follow, trust, obey, and believe. Christian faith and truth are tightly connected and inseparable: speaking of faith speaks of our Christian Truth, and speaking of our Truth speaks of our Christian faith. The longer we faithfully follow the truth of Jesus Christ, the stronger our faith in His faithfulness becomes. We are only able to be faithful because God is faithful and truthful. In a deeper sense, the beginning of faith is believing in the character of God. Charles Spurgeon said, "Faith is believing that Christ is who He said He is, and that He will do what He promises to do, and then expect this of Him."

God is Faithful.
(1 Corinthians 1:9 and 10:13; 2 Corinthians 1:18, NIV).

God is Truthful.
(John 3:33)

We use many synonyms for faith in our everyday language: trust, belief, confidence, optimism, hopefulness, hope, certainty, certitude, credit, assurance, sureness, credence, reliance, position of trust (responsibility, duty, obligation), and a belief in the reliability-truth-ability-strength of the object of faith.

We use many antonyms for faith in our everyday language: disbelief, distrust, doubt, uncertainty, mistrust, faithless, dishonesty, inconstancy, lying, treachery, unsteadiness, agnosticism, denial, misgiving, rejection, skepticism, suspicion, unbelief, rebel, reject, refuse, and disobey.

God is Love

(*hesed*, agape)

Biblically, what is love? The New Testament uses two different Greek words for "love": *agape*, the noun form, or *agapao*, the verb form, and *philia*, the noun form, and *phileo*, the verb form. *Agape* is most commonly used. It reportedly occurs 259 times in the New Testament, while *phileo* occurs only fifty-four times. Agape represents the covenant love of God for all human beings. Agape is representative of God's divine love, while *phileo* represents secular brotherly love. Biblically understanding the meaning and differences of these two Greek love words allows us to better comprehend God's way and will for us "on earth as it is in heaven."

God's love flows out of His faithfulness and grace. The Old Testament Hebrew word for love is *hesed*, which expresses God's faithful covenant love. This *hesed* commitment consists of self-giving, trust, deep affection, and joyful submission to the Law of the Covenant as an expression of love.

Agape, as used in the New Testament, expresses the essence of God and His character. Agape love is always divine, selfless, sacrificial, unconditional, and the greatest of all worldly loves. Agape love requires us to choose to die to self. It is tough, as it is promised to never fail or come to an end (1 Corinthians 13:8). Agape creates noble stories within God's epic story of love. Also, included within God's love is mercy, kindness, goodness, compassion, and care.

God is Love [Agape]
(1 John 4:8, 16 NIV)

Compare a biblical dictionary's definition of divine agape love to a secular dictionary's definition of love. Agape is a choice, while secular love is based on feelings. One stands strong, while the other blows with the wind.

Love is good when we choose to love what God loves as He directs us. Love turns evil when we choose to love what our Savior and Lord hates (idols and gods). Scripturally, we are called to guard our hearts and to be very careful of what we choose to love. We are also warned to be highly aware of our feelings that are strongly drawn towards the flesh and the world.

God is Righteous
He is Perfect by His Own Standard

Since God is perfect, it is impossible to define His righteousness by anything other than Himself. As to us, it is the status of rightness as judged by the standards of God's holy law which is derived from His holy character. God thinks, cares, and acts rightly. And as we learn to develop this character trait, we too will begin to do the same. Righteousness is many times in Scripture spoken of in terms of God's character, as in seek first the kingdom and His righteousness (Matthew 6:33).

God's righteous character flows out of His love, faithfulness, and grace. Righteousness includes blamelessness, right path, goodness, true, guide, word, kindness. Christian righteousness is about our right standing (justified), right thinking (orthodoxy), right caring (orthopathy), and right doing (orthopraxis) in Christ. Righteousness includes words and phrases such as self-control, discipline, temperance, taking life seriously, patience, good deeds, role model, honesty, and nobility. God's righteousness in the Amplified Version of the Bible describes the character traits of God that we are to aim at and strive after.

> But first and most importantly seek [aim at, strive after] His kingdom and His righteousness [His way of doing and being right—the attitude and character of God], and all these things will be given to you also."
> (Matthew 6:33, AMP)
>
> God is Righteous: For in the gospel the righteousness of God is revealed...
> (Romans 1:17 NIV)

God is Just

"The basis of morality as the right and fair way for people to relate to one another and to the world around them.... Justice is the basis from which we should act. ... In essence, justice is an active and life-giving virtue, which defends and promotes the dignity of every living person and is concerned for the Common Good insofar as it is the guardian of relations between individuals and peoples. Justice is at the same time a moral and a legal concept in that it fosters an equitable sharing of burdens and benefits. Justice makes whole and leads not to division, but reconciliation. At its deepest level, it is rooted in love and is tempered by mercy." (From a pastoral letter by the Catholic Bishops of England and Wales)

If, as mentioned above, justice is fairness, then how can God forgive sins and be considered just? In Romans 3:24-26, Paul tells us that we are "justified freely by his grace through the redemption"; by the Atonement he "demonstrates his justice"; and God is "just and the one who justifies." Since He is perfect and offered such a gift, who are we to complain?

God's justice flows out of His righteousness, love, faithfulness, and grace. The meaning of justice includes equity, fairness, truth, righteousness. Justice is about giving a person who is created in the image of God what is due. Justice lifts oppressive burdens and closes relational gaps to allow edifying resources to rightly flow towards a life of love, self-sufficiency, meaning, purpose, and wholeness. Justice will end in economic development but begins with human development.

God is just.
(2 Thessalonians 1:6, NIV)

God is Shalom
(wholeness, peace, joy)

> Love and Faithfulness meet together; Righteousness
> and Peace [Shalom] kiss each other. Faithfulness
> springs forth from the earth, and righteousness
> looks down from heaven.
> (Psalm 85:10-11, NIV)

Many times our English translations of the Old Testament
Hebrew and New Testament Greek do not carry the full
meaning of the original. One example is our English word
"peace." The following selection is taken from Efraim
Goldstein's article, "A Study on Biblical Concepts of Peace in
the Old and New Testaments" (www.jewsforjesus.org):

> What are the Biblical Concepts of Peace in the Old
> and New Testaments? Peace describes the state of
> those who love the Word of God (Psalm 119:165).
> The concept of peace expressed in the blessing of
> Aaron is found in Numbers 6:24, wherein it sums
> up all other blessings and is closely associated with
> the presence of God. Peace is the result of God's
> presence in a person's life as God is the source of
> peace (Psalm 85:8).

> What is the Old Testament Hebrew and New
> Testament Greek word meaning for our English

word "peace"? Peace in the Hebrew Old Testament is *shalom*. Peace in the Greek New Testament is *eirene*.

HEBREW: The Hebrew root word, *shalom*, denotes completion or wholeness. The general meaning of this word is of entering into a state of wholeness and unity, a restored relationship. It also conveys a wide range of nuances: fulfillment, completion, maturity, soundness, wholeness, harmony, tranquility, security, well-being, welfare, friendship, agreement, success and prosperity.

The word "shalom" occurs more than 250 times in Old Testament Scriptures (Tenach) and appears in 213 separate verses.

The classic Greek root, *eirene*, is the state of law and order that gives rise to the blessing of prosperity. It is also used to denote peaceful conduct toward others. The New Testament use of *eirene* remains firmly based in the Hebrew traditions of 'shalom' in the Old Testament (Tenach). It can describe both the content and the goal of all Christian preaching, since the message is called the Gospel of Peace (Ephesians 6:15).

The word *eirene* is found ninety-one times in the New Testament, twenty-four of which are in the Gospels.

What are some key concepts of "peace-shalom-eirene"? "Peace-shalom-eirene" is established by the God of peace (1 Corinthians 14:33; Romans 15:33;

Hebrews 13:20). "Peace-shalom-eirene" is linked with love (2 Corinthians 13:11). "Peace-shalom-eirene" from Jesus is different from the world's peace (John 16:33). According to the prophets, shalom will be an essential characteristic of the messianic kingdom; thus it is almost synonymous with messianic salvation (Ephesians 2:17). The promise of peace is through the Messiah (Prince of Peace)—His advent (Isaiah 9:6, Luke 2:10-14). And, the Prince of Peace, the Messiah, will come again.

And I heard a loud voice from heaven saying, "Behold, the tabernacle of God is with men, and He will dwell with them, and they shall be His people. God Himself will be with them and be their God." And God will wipe away every tear from their eyes; there shall be no more death, nor sorrow, nor crying. There shall be no more pain, for the former things have passed away. (Revelation 21:3-4)

Shalom, in the liturgy and in the transcendent message of the Christian scriptures, means more than a state of mind, of being or of affairs. Derived from the Hebrew root *shalam*, it means to be safe or complete, and by implication, to be friendly or to reciprocate. Shalom, as a term and message, seems to encapsulate a reality and hope of wholeness for the individual, within societal relations, and for the whole world. To say "joy and peace," meaning a state of affairs where there is no dispute or war, does not begin to describe the sense of the term. Completeness seems to be at the center of shalom, as we see in the meaning of the term itself.

The noun "shalom" means safe, well, and happy. On a more abstract application, its use points to welfare, as in health, prosperity, and peace. It is the verb form *shalam*, though, that provides a deeper understanding of this term in theology, doctrine, and liturgy. Literally translated, *shalam* signals to a state of safety, but figuratively it points to completeness. In its use in Scripture, *shalom* describes the actions that lead to a state of wholeness. *Shalom* seems not to merely speak of a state of affairs, but describes a *Shalom* Process, an activity, a movement towards fullness. Using the King James Version as reference, James Strong lists the rendering of *shalom* and *shalam*, among others, as meaning to make amends; to make good; to be (or to make) peace; to restore; and peace; prosperity; and wellness.

The use of shalom in the Scriptures always points towards that transcendent action of wholeness. The shalom process produces wholeness.

The Hebrew word and concept of shalom (*Strong's Concordance* # 7965) is not explicitly named in our Old Testament English translations, but is expressed in words and phrases such as wholeness, completeness, peace, joy, well-being, soundness, refreshed, rejoicing, Holy Mountain, delight, God's Dwelling, Kingdom of God, Garden of Eden, flourish, Songs of Joy, worship, praise, rest and metaphors such as still waters and green pastures. Shalom relates to our peace with God, self, and each other. It is God's gift of wholeness.

> May *ADONAI* give strength to his people! May
> *ADONAI* bless his people with *shalom*!
> (Psalm 29:11, Complete Jewish Bible)

In the New Testament, the Greek word equivalent for the Hebrew word shalom is *eirene* (*Strong's Concordance* #1515).

God is not a God of disorder but of peace [Eirene].
(1 Corinthians 14:33, NIV)

**GOD'S CHARACTER IS
GRACEFUL-FAITHFUL-LOVING-
RIGHT-JUST-SHALOM.**

Keith:

After my conversion, God showed me several aspects of His character—His grace, faithfulness, and love. He made me aware that over time these character traits could become mine.

While I accepted Jesus as my Savior and Lord, I cannot say that I was fully persuaded—at least, not in my head. I made a commitment to Jesus, but I felt like it was paper-thin. However, God knew my heart better than I did, and in His graciousness sent various signs over the next several months to convince my mind as well—all in the form of coincidences. A few may have seemed normal, but these came in such volume that I ultimately knew who provided them and realized why it was being done. The culmination came one Monday morning when I came to my office prepared to attend a hearing in Lafayette for 10 a.m. Looking at my calendar, I saw that I was in deep trouble as I also had a 10 a.m. hearing in Shreveport, a three-hour drive, and another in Baton Rouge, an hour away. After this, I asked for God's help. No sooner had I decided to call my opponent in Shreveport to get the hearing continued, than I got a call from the other attorney in Baton Rouge who needed a continuance. I readily agreed. I called Shreveport and spoke to the secretary. Her boss was out of town at another hearing. When I mentioned the hearing that morning, she asked if we could continue, and once again I agreed. As I hung up, my only response was to give thanks to God and to have complete confidence in my conversion, now having been fully persuaded.

It is important to understand the essence of God's character and that God's character traits are all interconnected and interdependent with each other for wholeness sake. The bookends of God's character are grace and shalom. Constantly meditate day and night on how these character traits interact as in one recipe. Oswald Chambers, in *My Utmost for His Highest*, October 31 Devotional, says, "God's character has to be clear in our minds. Faith in the Bible is faith in God against everything that contradicts Him—I will remain true to God's character whatever He may do. 'Though He slay me, yet will I trust Him.'"

It is because of the Character of God revealed to us in both the Word of God and the indwelling Spirit of God that we are able to faithfully and confidently make our stand and rightly act. When believers faithfully make a stand on the Character and Word of God, the power of God's Spirit is released.

Becoming holy is a sanctifying process which is accomplished and experienced through God developing His character traits of grace, faith, love, righteousness, justice, and shalom (peace, wholeness, joy) in us who are obediently being taught and trained. As these traits are daily worked out in our lives in harmony with both the Word and Spirit of God, they will become habitual and ultimately manifest themselves in our character. Each of these character traits are supported by, built on, and tightly connected to God's other character traits like a chain. All traits are inter-dependent with the other traits and are all united as one in Christ. The Christ-like character building process is often called the sanctification process.

> Because it is written, "YOU SHALL BE HOLY,
> FOR I AM HOLY."
> (1 Peter 1:16, NASB)

> Christ Jesus became like us, so that we might
> become like Him.
> (Unknown)

Please note: As we begin as followers, it will serve us well to have a vision of the character of God, beginning with the end in mind, and then to choose to allow God's Word and Spirit in us to begin His developmental process of building His character in us and helping us acquire His wisdom. In this developing and empowering process, we will find God's purpose for our lives. Here we will also discover our true identity in Christ, and not conform any longer to the image of the fallen world.

God's primary way to accomplish our Christ-like character development is love. By grace through faith we are freed and empowered to faithfully love and be loved. Faith is the key that turns on the powerful engine of the Holy Spirit and law in us. The character transforming pathway is obeying the Greatest Commandments to love; it begins and ends with faith empowered by the Spirit and guided by the Word of God. Gracefully stepping out in faithful love that is centered in Christ is the Great Transformer. On the other side of our faithful agape love is righteousness, justice, and shalom. Review and memorize God's six character traits.

> But those who wish to boast should boast in this alone: that they truly know me and understand that I am the Lord who demonstrates unfailing love and who brings justice and righteousness to the earth, and that I delight in these things. I, the Lord, have spoken!
> (Jeremiah 9:24, NLT)

> We are assured and know that [God being a partner in their labor] all things work together and are [fitting into a plan] for good to and for those who love God and are called according to [His] design and purpose. For those whom He foreknew [of whom He was aware and loved beforehand], He also destined from the beginning [foreordaining them] to be molded into the image of His Son [and share inwardly His likeness], that He might become the firstborn among many brethren.
> (Romans 8:28, AMPC)

Being conformed to the image and character of Christ Jesus is our Christian design, purpose, identity and destiny.

The biblical character of our God on earth, seen as being full of grace, faith (truth), love, righteousness, justice, and shalom (wholeness, peace and joy), produces the fruit identified in the scriptural lists of the Spirit's fruit. This fruit is the irresistible outcome of Christ's character. These good fruitful outcomes of the Spirit of God and the Word of God are God's work being done in and through Christ followers. It is His fruit. He breaks the soil of our hearts, plants the seeds, fertilizes, grows, and develops it all. Together these fruits create the irresistible virtues of Christ Jesus' character and His Kingdom that all humans deeply desire to abide in. These virtues create the beloved community where we desire to live, work, and raise our children and provide the nutritious soil all people are designed to grow up straight and strong in. These character traits, developed in the way of agape love, are reflective of whole people, whole families, whole churches, and whole communities, socially and economically. When we, individually and collectively, are in right and caring relationships with God, selves, and neighbors, the blessings of God are then able to freely flow from God, through His people, and then out to our family and others. All God's freeing and empowering graces are designed to flow down vertically and out horizontally in all directions through right and caring relationships. New Covenant grace creates Christ-like character that determines our destiny in the Kingdom of God. Thus, "Thy Kingdom come, Thy will be done on earth as it is in heaven."

But first *and* most importantly seek (aim at, strive after) His kingdom and His righteousness [His way of doing and being right—the attitude and character of God], and all these things will be given to you also.

(Matthew 6:33, AMP)

QUESTIONS

1. Why is it important to biblically know and have a vision?

2. What is God's stated purpose for every believer, according to Romans 8:28-29? Why? What does it mean?

3. Biblically describe the Character of God as described in Psalms.

4. As stated in Romans 12:2, what does it mean to renew one's mind? How does one renew the mind?

5. Select a character trait of God, and explain its importance and how it connects to other traits.

6. What two visions does Jesus teach us to seek (strive for, and aim at)? (Matthew 6:33)

7. Why is character so important?

8. Why is the grace of both the Word and Spirit of God foundationally important to a believer's growth? To the growth of the Family of God?

CHAPTER TWO

The Character
of the Kingdom of God

Nelson:

> An elderly mentor, Lowell Noble, stood in front of
> our retreat group and asked, "Beyond making Jesus
> the Lord and King of your life, can you biblically
> describe the Kingdom of God?" Everyone had an
> answer, but none could describe the biblical vision
> of the Kingdom of God. The group described some
> of its characteristics but could not deliver the fuller
> biblical understanding succinctly. Our group had no
> biblical vision of "Thy Kingdom Come"!

The King's kingdom vision is: "Thy Kingdom Come…"

> But seek the kingdom of God, and all these things
> shall be added to you.
> (Luke 12:31, NKJV)

How would you succinctly and biblically describe the
Kingdom of God on earth?

In the previous chapter, the character of God was biblically described as being full of

1) Grace,
2) Faith (in the Truth),
3) Love,
4) Righteousness,
5) Justice, and
6) Shalom.

God's purpose for believers to be lovingly conformed to the image and character of our Lord was also discussed. In this understanding, we are beginning with the end in mind by developing God's vision for our lives. There will probably be no surprise to discover that the biblical character of God is also reflected in the character of His Kingdom. The King's character permeates every aspect of the King's kingdom and His subjects.

> "For I know the plans I have for you," declares the Lord, "plans to prosper you and not to harm you, plans to give you hope and a future."
> (Jeremiah 29:11, NIV)

Reflect on the preceding verse and answer the following questions:

1) What does Jeremiah 29:11 say to you?
2) In this verse is the "you" singular or plural?
3) To whom is God actually speaking to?
4) Can you see that God is a God of community, as well as of the individual?

The Lord's Prayer begins with "Our Father," not "My Father." Even though the singular is true, the plural is God's bigger truth that can sometimes be hidden in our American culture that idolizes individualism.

What often begins with "me," ends with "we" in kingdom economics. To get from "here" to "there" we must have a vision of the "there" (the Kingdom of God on earth as in heaven), or we will end up someplace else. Vision is important, because in Proverbs 29:18, God tells us that where there is no vision people will perish (KJV), cast off restraint (NIV), and run wild (NLT). Possessing a biblical Kingdom vision is very important.

The Kingdom of God Vision

Note: Please do not consider this a "Kingdom-in-a-box," but the beginning of our struggle to envision and embrace the revealed character of our King and His Kingdom on earth as it is in heaven.

> Seek the shalom of the city where I have caused you
> to be carried away...for in the shalom thereof shall
> ye have shalom.
> (Jeremiah 29:7, Orthodox Jewish Bible)

> For the kingdom of God is not just a lot of talk; it is
> living by God's power."
> (1 Corinthians 4:20, NLT)

Paul describes the Kingdom of God and how it is produced:

> For God's kingdom does not consist of food and
> drink, but of righteousness, peace, and joy produced
> by the Holy Spirit.
> (Romans 14:17, ISV)

Paul further teaches believers to pursue these and the
other important Kingdom characteristics:

> Pursue righteousness, faithfulness, love, and shalom,
> with those who call on the Lord from a pure heart.
> (2 Timothy 2:22b, TLV)

Isaiah's Messianic Passages

The different Messianic passages in Isaiah (NIV) describe the
characteristics of the Kingdom of God as follows:

1) For to us a child is born, to us a son is given, and the
   government will be on his shoulders. And he will be
   called Wonderful Counselor, Mighty God, Everlasting
   Father, Prince of Peace. Of the increase of his
   government and peace there will be no end. He will
   reign on David's throne and over his kingdom,
   establishing and upholding it with justice and
   righteousness from that time on and forever.
   (Isaiah 9:6-7)

2) A shoot will come up from the stump of Jesse; from
   his roots a Branch will bear fruit. The Spirit of the
   LORD will rest on him— the Spirit of wisdom and of
   understanding, the Spirit of counsel and of power, the
   Spirit of knowledge and of the fear of the LORD—
   and he will delight in the fear of the LORD. He will

34

not judge by what he sees with his eyes, or decide by what he hears with his ears; but with <u>righteousness</u> he will judge the needy, with <u>justice</u> he will give decisions for the poor of the earth. He will strike the earth with the rod of his mouth; with the breath of his lips he will slay the wicked. <u>Righteousness</u> will be his belt and <u>faithfulness</u> the sash around his waist.
(Isaiah 11:1-5)

3) In <u>love</u> a throne will be established;
    in <u>faithfulness</u> a man will sit on it—one from the
    house of David—one who in judging seeks <u>justice</u>
    and speeds the cause of <u>righteousness</u>.
    (Isaiah 16:5)

4) So this is what the Sovereign LORD says: "See, I lay a
    stone in Zion, a tested stone, a precious cornerstone
    for a sure foundation; the one who <u>trusts (faith)</u> will
    never be dismayed. I will make <u>justice</u> the measuring
    line and <u>righteousness</u> the plumb line; hail will sweep
    away your refuge, the lie, and water will overflow your
    hiding place.
    (Isaiah 28:16-17)

5) Here is my servant, whom I uphold, my chosen one
    in whom I delight; I will put my <u>Spirit</u> on him and he
    will bring <u>justice</u> to the nations. He will not shout or
    cry out, or raise his voice in the streets. A bruised
    reed he will not break, and a smoldering wick he will
    not snuff out. In <u>faithfulness</u> he will bring forth
    <u>justice</u>; he will not falter or be discouraged till he
    establishes <u>justice</u> on earth. In his law the islands will
    put their hope.
    (Isaiah 42:1-4)

6) The <u>Spirit</u> of the Sovereign LORD is on me,
   because the LORD has anointed me
   to proclaim good news to the poor.
He has sent me to bind up the brokenhearted,
   to proclaim freedom for the captives
   and release from darkness for the prisoners, to
proclaim the year of the <u>LORD's favor</u>
   and the day of vengeance of our God,
to comfort all who mourn,
   and provide for those who grieve in Zion—
to bestow on them a crown of beauty
   instead of ashes,
the oil of joy
   instead of mourning,
and a garment of praise
   instead of a spirit of despair.
They will be called oaks of <u>righteousness</u>,
   a planting of the LORD
   for the display of his splendor.
They will rebuild the ancient ruins
             and restore the places long devastated;
they will renew the ruined cities
   that have been devastated for generations…
For I, the LORD, love <u>justice</u>;
         I hate robbery and wrongdoing.
In my <u>faithfulness</u> I will reward my people
   and make an everlasting covenant with them.
Their descendants will be known among the nations
   and their offspring among the peoples.
All who see them will acknowledge
   that they are a people the LORD has blessed.
(Isaiah 61:1-4, 8-9)

(Jesus' Mission Statement is found in verses 1-2 in Isaiah 61 and in Luke 4:18-19.)

Jesus describes important Kingdom characteristics in Matthew 23:13, 23b, NIV: "Woe to you, teachers of the law and Pharisees, you hypocrites! You shut the door of the kingdom of heaven in people's faces...But you have neglected the more important matters of the law—justice, mercy, and faithfulness. You should have practiced the latter, without neglecting the former."

As to the Kingdom, what does Jesus say are "the more important matters of the Law"?

> "Well said, teacher," the man replied. "You are right in saying that God is one and there is no other but him. To love him with all your heart, with all your understanding and with all your strength, and to love your neighbor as yourself is more important than all burnt offerings and sacrifices." When Jesus saw that he had answered wisely, he said to him, "You are not far from the kingdom of God..."
> (Mark 12:32, NIV)

What is Jesus' Way to the Kingdom?

Jesus said, "But first and most importantly seek (aim at, strive after) His kingdom and His righteousness [His way of doing and being right—the attitude and character of God], and all these things will be given to you also" (Matthew 6:33, AMP).

Jesus tells His followers first and foremost to seek, aim at, and strive for both our Father's Kingdom and His righteous character. This directive from Jesus requires a vision—a vision of the King and Kingdom that is revealed to us in Scripture.

Micah's Mandate: He has showed you, O man, what is good. And what does the LORD require of you? To act justly and to love mercy and to walk humbly with your God (Micah 6:8).

Let us begin with the end in mind by seeking a biblical vision of the King's Kingdom on earth by comparing the Kingdom Characteristics from Isaiah, Micah, Jesus, and Paul:

Isaiah:	Micah:	Jesus:	Paul:
1) _____	_____	_____	_____
2) _____	_____	_____	_____
3) _____	_____	_____	_____
4) _____	_____	_____	_____
5) _____	_____	_____	_____

Assignment: Create a one or two sentence Vision Statement of what the Kingdom of God on earth looks like biblically. Consider using the common character traits in Isaiah's Messianic passages, Jesus' Mission Statement in Luke 4:18-19 and Isaiah 61:1-2, Paul's description of the Kingdom in Romans 14:17, Micah and Jesus' Mandates, the Beatitudes,

Jesus' missional pathway and framework of the Greatest Commandments in Matthew 22:37-40, and the New Commandment in John 13:34-35.

Are the Kingdom Characteristics reflected in the Beatitudes? How do these values compare to Micah's Mandate?

Beatitudes

3 "Blessed are the poor in spirit, for theirs is the kingdom of heaven. (less of me, and more of God).
4 Blessed are those who mourn (able to see and mourn broken relationships, mourning the loss of love), for they will be comforted.
5 Blessed are the meek [humble, pride less, selfless], for they will inherit the earth.
6 Blessed are those who hunger and thirst for righteousness, for they will be filled.
7 Blessed are the merciful for they will be shown mercy.
8 Blessed are the pure in heart, for they will see God. (unmixed, unstained, free from falseness).
9 Blessed are the peacemakers, (shalom, reconcilers) for they will be called sons of God.
10 Blessed are those who are persecuted because of righteousness for theirs is the Kingdom of Heaven."
(Matthew 5:3-10, NIV)

Note: A Vision Statement describes the desired goal, product or destination. The Mission Statement provides the way to achieve the goal. The mission produces the product and is the roadmap to the destination. That is, the mission is the system that produces the desired product, the goal or vision.

> Vision: "Your kingdom come"
> Mission: "Your will be done...
> on earth as it is in heaven"
> (Matthew 6:10, NKJV)

In Our Father's Prayer, Jesus gives His Vision and Mission Statements for us.

The following are additional biblical pictures of the Kingdom of God to meditate on:

> But we are looking forward to the new heavens and new earth. He has promised, a world filled with God's righteousness.
> (2 Peter 3:13, NLT)

> Unfailing love and truth have met together. Righteousness and peace have kissed! Truth springs up from the earth, and righteousness smiles down from heaven. Yes, the Lord pours down his blessings. Our land will yield its bountiful harvest. Righteousness goes as a herald before him, preparing the way for his steps.
> (Psalm 85:10-13, NLT)

Read Psalm 85:10 in the NIV: "Love and faithfulness meet together." Compare how truth and faith are interchangeable in the NLT and NIV Old Testament Hebrew translations.

Faith and truth are related in that faith must be solidly anchored in an object, which is truth. Christian faith is anchored in the truth of Christ Jesus.

What will the Kingdom of God look like on Earth? When a society's people (communities, neighborhoods, families, businesses, churches, and the nation) are built up in the character of God's gracefulness, faithfulness in the Truth, love, righteousness, justice, and shalom (wholeness), His Kingdom will look like the picture painted for us in Isaiah 65:

> "See, I will create new heavens and a new earth. The former things will not be remembered, nor will they come to mind. But be glad and rejoice forever in what I will create, for I will create Jerusalem to be a delight and its people a joy. I will rejoice over Jerusalem and take delight in my people; the sound of weeping and of crying will be heard in it no more. Never again will there be in it an infant who lives but a few days, or an old man who does not live out his years; the one who dies at a hundred will be thought a mere child; the one who fails to reach a hundred will be considered accursed. They will build houses and dwell in them; they will plant vineyards and eat their fruit. No longer will they build houses and others live in them, or plant and others eat. For as the days of a tree, so will be the days of my people; my chosen ones will long enjoy the work of their hands. They will not labor in vain, nor will they bear children doomed to misfortune; for they will be a people blessed by the Lord, they and their descendants with them. Before

they call I will answer; while they are still speaking I will hear. The wolf and the lamb will feed together, and the lion will eat straw like the ox, and dust will be the serpent's food. They will neither harm nor destroy on all my holy mountain," says the Lord. (Isaiah 65: 17-25, NIV)

Question: Isaiah described a new community in Chapter 65 (above). In a visible and practical sense, what will the Kingdom of God look like on earth, according to Isaiah?
Discuss the following: joy (no weeping); long, healthy lives; home security and ownership; benefit from work; the chosen will enjoy their (sacred) work; bright futures for their children; blessed; God is near and hears; shalom and no harm or destruction.

How does one enter the Kingdom of God here on earth?

Generally speaking, the Kingdom of God is the "Rule of the King." Those who choose to live in the King's Kingdom now must also choose to live under the King's rule and commands. By nature, we humans do not want the King, or anyone else, to rule over us. We desire to please ourselves. Not until we experience a spiritual rebirth will we submit and commit ourselves to our King's Rule and enter into His Kingdom on earth as it is in heaven. Once in the Kingdom, His Word and Spirit in us will begin our transformation into our King's likeness and character. Our lives change and wisdom is found. The Kingdom of God is both present and future.

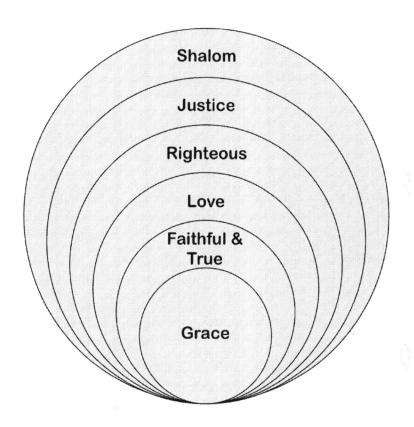

1. Why would the character of the King reflect the Kingdom of God? (In business, does the CEO or owner's character permeate the whole organization?)

2. What character traits does the King desire in His subjects?

3. What do faithful obedience and love have to do with the Kingdom of God? (see Matthew 22:37-40 and Mark 12:32-34) Can we love at the agape level without the New Covenant's grace of a transformed heart, indwelling Spirit, and Word?

How is the character of the King and Kingdom developed in a Christian? If we do not respond to the Word and to the Spirit's leading, over time we will stop hearing God's voice and eventually will put out the Spirit's fire. No desirable fruit will be produced. Let's make a habit of saying, "Yes, Lord!" This obedient attitude will stoke the coals and put fuel on the fire of the Spirit, allowing the Holy Spirit to burn ever brighter in our life—just by saying, "Yes, Lord." In faithfully doing what we are led to do, we will have a front row seat to watch God powerfully produce His fruit through and around us. So, "Do not quench the Spirit" (1 Thessalonians 5:19, NIV) with unfaithfulness, "and do not grieve the Holy Spirit of God" (Ephesians 4:30a, NIV). Make a daily habit of faithfully, obediently, trustingly, believingly following Christ's Spirit and Word. Then behold the fruit of His character being developed in you. Christian character development is explained further in Chapter 3.

QUESTIONS

1. In Isaiah 42:1, the prophet describes God's ultimate goal for His Kingdom on earth. Describe it. How is it being achieved?

2. Based on the Scripture cited, it appears some of the Kingdom characteristics, in addition to love, are faithfulness, righteousness, justice, shalom (wholeness, peace, joy). Select the characteristics you think the Holy Spirit desires to develop in you today and/or has begun to develop. Describe your development process.

3. In showing the disciples how to pray, what vision was Jesus painting when he said "…your Kingdom come…"? Is this an end times vision and/or for the "here and now"?

4. Since faith must always have an object, what is the object of your Christian faith? What do you love most? Do you recognize things that you love that God does not? What are you doing about that?

5. When God's Kingdom comes to earth as it is in heaven, how can one enter it?

CHAPTER THREE

Christian Character Development

Christ-like Character Development: The Christian pathway towards character development appears to be all over the map. It ranges from the believers who are unaware of, or who feel there is no need for, righteous character development to the other extreme of a legalistic obsession toward character development. The Bible has a much higher roadway toward character development that exists between these two extremes.

Who are you really? People are generally a combination of who they think they are and who the world tells them they are, but the reality is found only in our Creator who can rightly tell us who we truly are and created to be.

God created man in His image (Genesis 1:27). This profound verse reveals who we truly were meant to be before the Fall. Since the Fall, this image has been constantly tarnished, contorted, and confused into something that man is not, a false identity. The flesh, the world, and Satan feed and breed this false identity. Our false identity has now become normalized. Jesus Christ incarnationally came to reveal who we truly are by reconciling and redeeming what has been lost and broken in the Kingdom. He came to take the dull, false tarnish off our original silver identity. Jesus also came to model to the transformed and regenerated believers who we truly are as created in His image. Christ's Spirit and Word tells us that we are not who we think we are, or who the world tells us we are! After placing believers back on His shining silver tray, Christ's indwelling Spirit, in harmony with the Word, begins peeling back the many false layers and aligning our true nature with His untarnished character. As God's nature and character are all one and the same, our nature and character are to become unified too. After all, it is in becoming like Christ Jesus that we ultimately discover who we are uniquely created to be, and that gives us meaning and purpose. In essence, Christ followers are becoming who they truly already are in His image.

What Is Character?

Character is who we are and who we are becoming. Character is evidenced by our thinking, caring, and doing. Character is shown in what we do when nobody's looking. Character is reflective of what we have chosen to love and value the most in our lives. If we choose to love our Lord Christ Jesus the most, then we will slowly begin to resemble Him. Our nature and character will become closer and closer aligned with Christ's likeness. If we choose to love the world the most, then we will resemble the world. But in choosing to love the world, our true nature created in the image of God and the world's character will be at odds with each other. Whether we choose to love Christ's Way or the world's way, our habitual choice will ultimately determine our character and destiny.

The short definition of the Greek word *charaktér* (*Strong's Concordance*, #5481) is being an exact reproduction.

In Scripture, character is explicitly spoken of most often in the Amplified Versions of the Bible (in AMP, 71 times and in AMPC, 37 times). There are many Greek words that describe character. By comparing the many different Bible versions with the AMP version, God's Character is translated and spoken of in Scripture in many equivalent words and phrases: conformed-molded into His image-pattern, His ways, Your Name, revealed You, make You known, maturity, sons of God, perfect, perfecting, perfection, righteousness, (you will be made) complete, fully restored, new self, restoration repair, mature Christians, true Christian maturity, spiritual maturity, improvement, clothed yourself with Christ, live a life worthy of the calling, walk in Him, live in Him, rooted in Him, live in Christ Jesus the Lord, God's seed, participate in the divine nature, God likeness, Christ likeness, whole, image of God.

Meditate on these Scriptural synonyms for "character."

What Is God's Purpose for Those Who Love Him?

And we know that in all things God works for the good of those who love him, who have been called according to his purpose. [And His purpose is] For those God foreknew he also predestined to be conformed to the image of his Son, that he might be the firstborn among many brothers and sisters. And those he predestined, he also called; those he called, he also justified; those he justified, he also glorified. (Romans 8:28-30, NIV)

Paul's use of "glorified" includes the process of sanctification and refers to developing Christ's character likeness in us. Thus, God's glorification process has two sides (justification/salvation + sanctification) that conform followers to His Son's image.

Let us remember that the glorious "Son is the image of the invisible God, the firstborn over all creation…" (Colossians 1:15a, NIV). And Christ followers are now purposed by God to be gloriously conformed to Christ Jesus' image.

Why Does God Purpose Believers to Become Christ-Like in Character?

In harmony with the King, Kingdom people are to have Kingdom character on earth as it is in heaven.

How is Christian character developed?

> And we all, with unveiled face, continually seeing as
> in a mirror the glory of the Lord, are progressively
> being transformed into His image from [one degree
> of] glory to [even more] glory, which comes from
> the Lord, [who is] the Spirit.
> (2 Corinthians 3:18, AMP)

Our Christ-like character development, like all development, is a progressive experience (Galatians 4:19; Philippians 3:21; 1 John 3:2). We know about Christ Jesus in Bible studies. We begin knowing Christ Jesus through obedience. The more we lovingly follow and know our Lord, the more we will become like Him. And those obediently led by the indwelling Spirit are children of God and co-heirs with Christ and will share in His glory (Romans 8:11-17).

Christ is the "firstborn among many brothers and sisters" (Romans 8:29b, NIV) in the King's family who are being conformed to His character. All this happens so that Christ is both glorified and multiplied in all aspects of life.

Christian character development begins and ends with our regenerated hearts (New Covenant grace). It is a two-sided process: Salvation and Sanctification (S2). Simply stated, the way of Christian character development begins with choosing to love our Savior and Lord more than anyone or anything else. What we love most will become our thoughts, which will become our words, which will become our actions, which will become our habits, which will become our character, which will determine our destiny. That is, our character is determined by what we have chosen to love the most. God directs us to love Him most for this, His purpose.

This character-building process requires daily teaching and training. By creating the good habits, the bad character habits will begin falling away to reveal our true identity. The Word of God is very important for us to love, eat, and digest, as we habitually do with food. "Jesus said, 'Man does not live by bread alone, but on every word that comes from the mouth of God'" (Matthew 4:4, NIV). In having a daily hunger for and consumption of God's word, believers will begin to think like our Lord, especially when God's Word drops from our minds and into our hearts. In His Word and Spirit, followers are being taught, rebuked, corrected, and trained in right standing, right caring, right thinking, and right doing (2 Timothy 3:16-17). Character development requires that believers go under God's habitual daily teaching, guiding, and training program which may not be comfortable and may even be painful. As the saying goes, "No pain, no gain."

> Therefore, since we have been justified by faith, we have peace with God through our Lord Jesus Christ. Through him we have also obtained access by faith into this grace in which we stand, and we rejoice in hope of the glory of God.
> (Romans 5:1-2, ESV)

The above verse represents the salvation side of the Christian life (released). And beyond salvation there is more...

> More than that, we rejoice in our sufferings, knowing that suffering produces endurance, and endurance produces character, and character produces hope, and hope does not put us to shame, because God's love has been poured into our hearts through the Holy Spirit who has been given to us."
> (Romans 5:3-5, ESV)

The above verses represent the sanctification side of the Christian life (empowered). We who love our Lord are being "remade" in His character-likeness by persevering through our suffering by the love of God and with His Holy Spirit in our hearts! (God's "suffering pathway" to character development and hope is the pathway of tough-love, a point that Christians quite often miss.)

> It helps to keep in mind the two-sided reality of the Christian life. On the one hand, we are complete in Christ (our acceptance with Him is secure). On the

other hand, we are growing in Christ (we are becoming more and more like Him). At one and the same time we have the status of kings and the duties of slaves. We feel both the presence of Christ and the pressure of sin. We enjoy the peace that comes from being made right with God, but we still face daily problems that often help us grow. If we remember these two sides of the Christian life, we will not grow discouraged as we face temptations and problems. Instead, we will learn to depend on the power available to us from Christ, who lives in us by the Holy Spirit.
(note in *Tyndale's Life Application Study Bible* on Romans 5:1-5)

Once being justified by grace through faith, believers stand and rejoice in the hope of God's glory. In Romans 5:3-5, we are also promised that there is more. We are to rejoice in our suffering! Believers are promised that our suffering will produce endurance and our endurance will produce Christ-like character which will produce hope on the other side of our suffering. Along with Christ-like character we will also gain hope on the other side of our struggle because God's agape love has been poured into our hearts by the Holy Spirit in us! We are promised that suffering is God's pathway to developing His character. In our *K2* language today, we call this development pathway tough-love.

In Scripture, Christ followers are promised suffering (tough-love). Paul reminded his church, "that we must suffer [tough-love] many hardships to enter the Kingdom of God" (Acts

14:22, NLT). Jesus tells His disciples, "If they persecuted me, they will also persecute you" (John 15:20, ESV). Peter tells Christians, "My dear friends, do not be surprised at the painful test you are suffering, as though something unusual were happening to you" (1 Peter 4:12, GNT). And Paul tells Timothy, "Yes, and those who decide to please Christ Jesus by living godly lives will suffer at the hands of those who hate him" (2 Timothy 3:12, TLB).

In our faithful Christian walk, suffering and struggling are to be expected and there is no place for the victim narrative of bondage and powerlessness. Suffering simply comes with life, especially the Christian life. Yet, followers are released and empowered to rejoice in our suffering, not because we like suffering or deny suffering, but because we know that God uses our suffering and satanic attacks to grow in us His Son's character. And...

> After you have suffered for awhile, God Himself will make you perfect. He will keep you in the right way. He will give you strength. He is the God of all loving-favor and has called you through Christ Jesus to share His shining-greatness forever."
> (1 Peter 5:10, NLV)

Beyond God's tough-love character developing process, Jesus Christ's resurrection shows the great power of God by overcoming death. In the cross and resurrection, we are faithfully promised victory and given a hope and love that will not fail. So, let us never allow ourselves to fall into our old habits of playing the victim. We have a great hope on the other side of suffering and tough-love. In Christ's loving, freeing, and empowering grace, we will humbly stand as victors.

> "Despite all these things, overwhelming victory is ours through Christ, who loved us."
> (Romans 8:37, NLT)

So, instead of always trying to "fix" one another's struggles, we should embrace each other's struggles in the here and now. After all, it is on the far side of our Christian suffering and tough-love that followers are promised to become stronger in character and completeness.

> Dear brothers, is your life full of difficulties and temptations? Then be happy, for when the way is rough, your patience has a chance to grow. So let it grow, and don't try to squirm out of your problems. For when your patience is finally in full bloom, then you will be ready for anything, strong in character, full and complete.
> (James 1:2-4, TLB)

Like our coaches tell their teams, "No pain, no gain," our suffering is the tough-love pathway towards our Christ-like character development. This seems odd to an immature, untrained, and possibly wounded believer, but wisdom is gained on the far side of our struggles. This tough-love training is understood by the mature believer.

> Being punished isn't enjoyable while it is happening—it hurts! But afterwards we can see the result, a quiet growth in grace and character.
> (Hebrews 12:11, TLB)

Tough love does not feel loving, but it is the most loving way of human development and empowerment. Like Jesus Christ mercy is to be applied when the person in front of you is bleeding to death. Like the Holy Spirit tough-love development is to be immediately applied when the bleeding stops and God's development that empowers begins.

But you may say, "Life is good. I have no struggles or any suffering! How am I to mature in Christ-likeness without any struggle or suffering?" We are told in Romans 12:1 that our true act of worship is to offer our bodies as living sacrifices holy and pleasing to God. Offering our bodies as a living sacrifice for others reflects Jesus' suffering and offering of His body for all people. In Jesus' obedient offering, He nobly defines and models true agape love for mankind. John tells us that there is no greater love than agape (John 15:13). Agape love requires a dying to self…giving place to God and others before self. Faithful believers are promised to mature in Christ-like character along this sacrificial agape pathway. You may say, "Heck, I cannot love at this level," and you are right in your confession. But according to the guidance of the Word and indwelling power of the Spirit in our transformed hearts, we are equipped in faith to boldly and strongly enter the pain of others. Development and empowerment is not about doing "for," but doing "with" and alongside our neighbors, as Christ's Spirit is always alongside and in us. We enter their struggles, not by fixing their struggle, but by embracing it. As we become friends in this process, their pain becomes our pain. This is where followers create the noble sacrificial stories within God's epic story of love. In sacrificial agape love, we are promised to become like our great Lover, and people will know us by our love (John 13:35). When we embrace the character-building journey of "dying to self," "dying to live," and "taking up our cross daily," Scripture begins to take on deeper meaning, and we begin acquiring wisdom and truly begin to rightly love even ourselves (Proverbs 19:8, NLT).

The Agape Way quickly brings a believer to the end of self-sufficiency. Before I am empowered to love at the agape level, I must first confess my inadequacies and prayerfully stand on God's Word and rely on God's Spirit to love through me. A faithful person must go down to a confessed powerless place before receiving God's uplifting power. Even before I can become wise, I must first confess my weaknesses at the feet of Christ. God's way up is down. Before Christ-like character can begin its development in me, I must confess how far short I fall of God's glory, and ask Him to develop in me His character. God's Agape Way of development is the best and quickest way one comes to the end of "self" and begins living the abundant life in the power of Christ. Our Lord desires this close trusting relationship with us, and He promises us that His yoke is light (Matthew 11:28-30) and in our weakness, we are made strong.

> And He said to me, "My grace is sufficient for you, for My strength is made perfect in weakness." Therefore most gladly I will rather boast in my infirmities, that the power of Christ may rest upon me.
> (2 Corinthians 12:9, NKJV)

Acquiring wisdom is like the wise builder in Luke 6:46-49 who hears Jesus' words and puts them into practice. The wise builder built his house in God's Way and "When a flood came, the torrent struck that house but could not shake it, because it was well built" (Luke 6:48b, NIV). Jesus spoke about the results of the foolish builder who heard Jesus' Words, but did not put them into practice. The insane and foolish build with only the good weather in mind, and not the tumultuous weather. The foolish builder built his structure such that "The moment the torrent struck that house, it collapsed and its destruction was complete" (Luke 6:49b, NIV). The wise builder does not build for the beautiful days, but for the stormy tumultuous days. Christians are called to wisely build our Christ-like character on the Rock that will stand whatever the flesh, the world, and Satan throw at us.

Here are some "character" Scriptures to read, meditate on, and compare with synonyms in other Bible versions:

> But first and most importantly seek (aim at, strive after) His kingdom and His righteousness [His way of doing and being right—the attitude and character of God], and all these things will be given to you also.
> (Matthew 6:33, AMP)

> (Jesus said) "I have made Your Name known to them and revealed Your character and Your very Self, and I will continue to make [You] known, that the love which You have bestowed upon Me may be in them [felt in their hearts] and that I [Myself] may be in them."
> (John 17:26 AMPC)

For all of you who were baptized into Christ [into a spiritual union with the Christ, the Anointed] have clothed yourselves with Christ [that is, you have taken on His characteristics and values].
(Galatians 3:27, AMP)

We know that in all things God works for good with those who love him, those whom he has called according to his purpose. Those whom God had already chosen he also set apart to become like his Son, so that the Son would be the first among many believers.
(Romans 8:28-29, GNT)

(Jesus said) "You, therefore, must be perfect [growing into complete maturity of godliness in mind and character, having reached the proper height of virtue and integrity], as your heavenly Father is perfect."
(Matthew 5:48, AMPC)

Yet wisdom is vindicated and shown to be right by all her children [by the lifestyle, moral character, and good deeds of her followers].
(Luke 7:35, AMP)

So I, the prisoner for the Lord, appeal to you to live a life worthy of the calling to which you have been called [that is, to live a life that exhibits godly character, moral courage, personal integrity, and mature behavior—a life that expresses gratitude to God for your salvation].
(Ephesians 4:1, AMP)

And by that same mighty power he has given us all the other rich and wonderful blessings he promised; for instance, the promise to save us from the lust and rottenness all around us, and to give us his own character.
(2 Peter 1:4, TLB)

May you always be filled with the fruit of your salvation—the righteous character produced in your life by Jesus Christ—for this will bring much glory and praise to God.
(Philippians 1:11, NLT)

The Son radiates God's own glory and expresses the very character of God, and he sustains everything by the mighty power of his command.
(Hebrews 1:3a, NLT)

Just as iron sharpens iron, a person sharpens the character of his friend.
(Proverbs 27:17, CJB)

For this reason, I fall on my knees before the Father, from whom every family in heaven and on earth receives its character.
(Ephesians 3:14-15, CJB)

Now you must tell them the sort of character which should spring from sound teaching.
(Titus 2:1, PHILLIPS)

Therefore as you have received Christ Jesus the Lord, walk in [union with] Him [reflecting His character in the things you do and say—living lives that lead others away from sin].
(Colossians 2:6, AMP)

[He is] always striving for you in his prayers, praying with genuine concern, [pleading] that you may [as people of character and courage] stand firm, [spiritually mature] and fully assured in all the will of God.
(Colossians 4:12b, AMP)

We also pray for this, that you be made complete [fully restored, growing and maturing in godly character and spirit—pleasing your heavenly Father by the life you live].
(2 Corinthians 13:9b, AMP)

Paul told believers to not be conformed to the systems of this world, but be transformed into the knowing of God's system (Romans 12:2, AMP). Jesus warned that humans cannot follow and love two gods at the same time (Matthew 6:24). Believers are to prayerfully and habitually stay in step with the Spirit of God, not in step with Satan, the ruler of the worldly. Paul writes, "Since we live by the Spirit, let us keep in step with the Spirit" (Galatians 5:25, NIV).

The fallen world continually attempts to stamp its character on us by modifying our human behavior through different types of self-help works, programs, lectures, and other things that have no real power over our stronger flesh desires. God defines Himself—His character—on a much higher heavenly plane. This is a divine level that challenges believers to live above their earthly plane and faithfully trust God's Word and empowering Spirit in us to do His good works. Our humble and daily reliance on God's guidance and His loving power in us is what ultimately develops Christ's character in us that produces the fruit of His vine and requires His tough-love pruning, or "vineology" (John 15:1-17). Character is revealed by its fruit (Luke 6:43-45). The Wise Builder will come to Christ, hear Him, and then apply His Words to his life (Luke 6:47). The wise builder's character is then revealed by the storm (Luke 6:46-49).

In choosing to daily rely on Christ's power in us to do His Will, we know it is God carrying the load and not us. We only need to courageously show up in the pursuit of all character-building relationships.

Keith:

> After our grandson finished his freshman year of high school with four D's and one F, my wife and I became very concerned. His mother and father had never married and were continuously at odds with each other, resulting in the boy being pulled in different and confusing directions. My wife located a boarding school about three hours away which looked promising. After our grandson agreed to consider the change, the four of us visited the school and met with the administration. Upon returning home, both our grandson and his mom believed the change was a good idea, but his dad would hear nothing of it. Since they shared custody,

this presented a big problem. I enlisted the aid of several Christian men, and we began praying that God would change his dad's heart, but over the next few weeks there was no movement. His mom and I then engaged a lawyer to get a change of custody (Apparently my trust in God was not complete, and I felt that I could assist in affecting the outcome). But over the summer, with such an erratic schedule (judges do take vacations) our earliest hearing date was set for September 7, two and a half weeks after school was to begin. While the school was willing to work with him, I was not confident my grandson could catch up. The week before school was scheduled to begin, his dad, who is a Christ follower, called me to say the Holy Spirit had touched his heart, and he did not want to stand in the way of a good education for his son. Prayer was answered, and none of my legal efforts contributed to the outcome. In fact, I saw that I was still resistant to God's development of His character in me. Amen.

Thus, the Divine Character Builder, the Holy Spirit that we receive through our new birth in Christ is a free gift of grace that frees and empowers. But what character we develop out of God's grace is *our* daily and progressive choice to faithfully accept or not. God's desire is for us to faithfully build spiritual habits in harmony with His word and Spirit that are promised to lovingly develop our character in Christ, our True Vine.

In 2 Peter 1:1-9, NIV, Peter speaks of participating in God's divine nature by adding to our faith, goodness, knowledge, self-control, perseverance, godliness, brotherly kindness, and love so as to be effective and productive. This is stated a little differently in The Living Bible.

> From: Simon Peter, a servant and missionary of Jesus Christ. To: All of you who have our kind of faith. The faith I speak of is the kind that Jesus Christ our God and Savior gives to us. How precious it is, and how just and good he is to give this same faith to each of us. Do you want more and more of God's kindness and peace? Then learn to know him better and better. For as you know him better, he will give you, through his great power, everything you need for living a truly good life: he even shares his own glory and his own goodness with us! And by that same mighty power he has given us all the other rich and wonderful blessings he promised; for instance, the promise to save us from the lust and rottenness all around us, and to give us his own character. But to obtain these gifts, you need more than faith; you must also work hard to be good, and even that is not enough. For then you must learn to know God better and discover what he wants you to do. Next, learn to put aside your own desires so that you will become patient and godly, gladly letting God have his way with you. This will make possible the next step, which is for you to enjoy other people and to like them, and finally you will grow to love them deeply. The more you go on in this way, the more you will grow strong spiritually and become fruitful and useful to our Lord Jesus Christ. But anyone who fails to go

63

after these additions to faith is blind indeed, or at least very shortsighted and has forgotten that God delivered him from the old life of sin so that now he can live a strong, good life for the Lord.
(2 Peter 1:1-9, TLB)

Peter speaks of a different kind of faith than our secular human faith. Peter states, "The faith I speak of is the kind that Jesus Christ our God and Savior gives to us" (2 Peter 1:1, TLB). We humans were not born with this kind of faith, it is a gift from our "just and good" Jesus Christ. In verse 2, Peter asks that if we desire more and more of Christ's peace and kindness, then we need to learn how to know Him better. In the faithful process of knowing Him better, He will powerfully give us everything we need, as we need it, to live a truly good life. Is Peter saying that God has given us "character" as a gift? No, it is not a gift as we normally think. Some gifts are given immediately, while other gifts like character are developed over time, as Peter alludes in the above verses. Character is not so much an instant gift as is our salvation and the indwelling Holy Spirit. Character-building is a developmental process, not a "zapping." Our character development process begins with our conscious choice to allow the Spirit and Word to control our lives to the extent that they develop and reflect the character of Christ in all we think and do. We are called to choose to become true partakers of Christ's Divine Nature in us and reflect His character of the Kingdom of God on earth to all God's good, albeit now tarnished, creation. God's process that develops Christ's character in us is ultimately a gift that is being developed by grace through faith that is expressed in agape love. In the process our Savior and Lord is always with us and in us.

God's Iron Rule of Character Development:

Just as the "Iron Rule" tells us not to do for others what they can do for themselves, so God will not do for us what He has freed and empowered us to do for ourselves!

Please note that God's character is, of course, much higher than secular man's highest understanding of His character. Even though the character traits may have the same name, like love, they have two totally different meanings. The secular *phileo* love reflects a natural brotherly type love based on common affections and feelings and is totally different from agape, the sacrificial selfless love based on choice. The secular love is within human power and is natural, while divine sacrificial love is only accomplished in the power of God's Spirit in us who believe. Thus, fruitful Christians will always look different than the world by their faith in the truth of Jesus Christ that is expressed in sacrificial love.

Peter is telling us to intentionally choose to allow God to add to our faith (2 Peter 1:9) and to develop His divine character in us, allowing our Savior and Lord to have His Way with us. This divine character development exists beyond our first step of faith. Faith is the "key" that ignites the powerful engine of the Holy Spirit within. Our continuous and faithful obedience to the Law of love is God's "Road-Way" towards our Christ-likeness character development: putting on the new self in Christ.

Your hearts and minds must be made completely new, and you must put on the new self, which is created in God's likeness and reveals itself in the true life that is upright and holy.
(Ephesians 4:23-24, TEV)

Holy (*hagios*, Greek) means sacred, set apart by God, for God. *Strong's Concordance* #40 states that *hagios* means "likeness of nature with the Lord." It means to be "different from the world," because we are to become "like the Lord," that is set apart, different, distinguished, and distinct—holy in His character likeness.

Don't let your character be moulded by the desires of your ignorant days, but be holy in every department of your lives, for the one who has called you is himself holy. The scripture says: "Be holy, for I am holy."
(1 Peter 1:15:16, PHILLIPS)

Our aiming at becoming Christ-like in character is most important and foundational to "Thy Kingdom Come, Thy Will Be Done On Earth..." Becoming Christ-like in character is God's purpose for all believers in the Family of God (Romans 8:28-29). Let us move on past the door of salvation and get on with conforming into the image of Christ.

So come on, let's leave the preschool finger-painting exercises on Christ and get on with the grand work of art. Grow up in Christ. The basic foundational truths are in place: turning your back on "salvation by self-help" and turning in trust toward God;

baptismal instructions; laying on of hands; resurrection of the dead; eternal judgment. God helping us, we'll stay true to all that. But there's so much more. Let's get on with it!
(Hebrews 6:1-3, MSG)

Becoming the Living Proof of a Loving God to a Broken and Hurting World (becoming noble)

So, who are you, individually and collectively?

Genesis 1:27, NIV, states "So God created mankind in his own image, in the image of God he created them; male and female he created them." We know by God's word that mankind was originally created in the image and likeness of God! This truth is both foundational and dignifying. This profound statement is our true identity as we were originally created by God. In the Garden, God only desired obedience; there was no sacrifice. Then there was the Fall of Mankind from God's glory (Genesis 3:1-24). Now all people are sinners and fall short of the glory of God (Romans 3:23). Our now tarnished identity, sinful nature, is being constantly fed and bred by the lies and deceit of the flesh, the world, and Satan. Christ Jesus came to destroy these works of the devil (1 John 3:8), and "remake" His followers into our original glory and God's original design for us. Christ followers are now becoming who we truly are in Christ. And, this process includes the whole family of God, where many brothers and sisters are purposely being remade in His character likeness. This sanctifying-glorifying holy process strips away the false self and puts on the true self in Christ. Our transformation comes through the agape process of giving place to God and others before self, a dying to self, a carrying our cross daily, an offering of our bodies as living sacrifices. This Agape Way connects our physical being to our true spiritual being as one and the same with no dichotomy. God has always demanded obedience, while our fallen sin nature demands sacrifice to get real. Without sacrificial, agape love there will remain a great separation between the physical and the spiritual. Without the agape way, there will be no noble stories or fruit or maturity in Christ—only secular Christians who generally cause more harm than good.

Our true identity in Christ-likeness is being developed and discovered through much teaching, rebuking, correcting, and training in righteousness (2 Timothy 3:16-17). In God's tough-love training and suffering process, we must remain centered in Christ, centered in both His word and Spirit, where we are promised to be released, transformed, and empowered. "The reign of God is within you" (Luke 17:21, YLT). We are becoming who we are meant to be—who God originally designed and created us to be. The old false self is gone, while the new true self has arrived (1 Corinthians 5:17). For His glory, we are glorified.

While being Christ's Ambassadors (2 Corinthians 5:20), our Christ-like character will also free and empower us for the battle fronts.

QUESTIONS

1. Before coming to Christ, how would you have answered the question, "Who are you?" How would you answer it now?

2. As to Romans 5:1-5, describe the Two-Sided Reality of the Christian Life.

3. Since Christian character development is a blend of God's grace and our choices, what are some of the things Peter tells us to consider in so choosing (2 Peter 1:1-9)?

4. As to the "Iron Rule" what are the kinds of things God will do and what are the things we are empowered to do as applied to the character development process?

5. In Scripture, describe God's tough-love process of character development.

6. Why is tough-love required in our human development-empowerment (teaching to fish, own, and care for the pond) as opposed to mercy?

CHAPTER FOUR

The Battle Fronts

Nelson:

"God saw everything that He had made, and indeed it was very good" (Genesis 1:31, NKJV). Everything is created by God and is made very good, but man can quickly take something good and make it evil when he chooses to love it more than God. Biblically, these displaced loves are called idols, little "g" gods, and result in sin. When we have chosen to love anything more than God, we are idolaters and sinners. We've missed God's mark. Our idols and sin signal misplaced loves that we consciously place before and above our Lord Jesus Christ. These misplaced loves cause us to break relationship with God, others, and even ourselves. To get a hold on our idols, we will do anything over God and others. Ultimately, our idols will hold us back— individually and collectively—from growing up in Christ-likeness and will result in our being bad witnesses for Christ.

During my first year at our inner-city ministry, I just could not get our little under-resourced, unchurched children out of my mind. They began occupying my every thought, day and night. One night I was again wondering out loud about certain young boys and how to best touch their little minds and hearts. My wife abruptly said, "I'm so tired of hearing about Bridge Ministry!"

Boom! My first thoughts were, "Doesn't she know this is God's work!" Then I realized with horror that I had made an idol out of our inner-city ministry. I had turned God's work into my god's work. I had placed my ministry and calling in front of not only God, but ahead of my wife too. Idolatry's red flag of broken relationships hit me in the face. Idolatry is subtly and easily normalized, especially in our American culture. People can create an idol out of anything or anyone and need training in both Word and Spirit learn to discern. When Christ followers are no different than the world, be assured our love idols are flourishing. Anyway, as faithfully promised, God's Word and Spirit immediately began rebuking and correcting me back to His right and loving pathway. God's system of love wins.

Professor Peter Drucker, one of the twentieth century's most brilliant minds on business management practices, said, "Every System is perfectly designed to produce the product it produces." Systems produce products (*K2 Series, Book One*, Chapter One, page 3). Whether good or bad, every system is perfectly designed to produce the product it produces.

Our Savior and Lord desires His Family, individually and collectively, to reflect more and more of His character and that of the Kingdom. For God's glory, believers are to be conformed to His likeness, and not to the world's likeness. God the Father sent His Son. His Son sent the Spirit. The indwelling Spirit now sends the Family of God, the Church, to reflect His glorious light.

As mentioned in Chapter 1 of Book 1, Christians are called to bring light and order to a dark and chaotic world. The Church is to be the light in the darkness, but many will love the darkness and hate the light.

Thus sets the battle line between a person's choice either to love the darkness or to love the light. This spiritual battle is for our hearts, and it is one which Christians need to be able to discern and for which they need to be trained and equipped.

Is the Church, or the church, (large "C" and small "c") living up to its potential? If not, what holds Christians back from being conformed to the image and character of Christ Jesus? What dims the Light?

Frequently, people are held back by oppressive events in their lives that are beyond their control. These oppressive forces can cause deep wounds that many people carry without knowing it. Many times these wounds are normalized in our minds, our culture, and our churches and go unrecognized.

Without going into detail here, these wounds can be generally seen as absent-parent wounds, overbearing-parent wounds, all-alone wounds, and the one wound all people are born with, the depravity wound.

The depravity wound is our being born separated from God due to the Fall. Jesus said:

> "The Spirit of the Lord is upon Me, Because He anointed Me to preach the gospel to the poor. He has sent Me to proclaim release to the captives, And recovery of sight to the blind, To set free those who are oppressed, To proclaim the favorable year of the Lord."
> (Luke 4:18-19, NASB)

Jesus came to heal our broken relationships that hold us back. Mother Teresa basically said that our deepest needs and desires are to be loved and to love. We generally get the "to be loved" part of her equation (especially by God), but we might not be so much aware of our God-designed need "to love." To possibly understand how we are created to love and worship, consider the many things that we may choose to love more than God: alcohol, drugs, sex, money, power, position, nature, animals, sports, and work. Whatever we choose to love more than what God directs us to love—God and our neighbors—will become an idol or a god. The battle is between our love choice for either Light or Darkness. The heart is the battle field, thus making our heart most important to God (and Satan).

Our tendency to place certain things above or before God is important. Thus, God speaks of idolatry in the very first two of the Ten Commandments:

> You shall have no other gods before me.
> You shall not make for yourself an image in the form of anything in heaven above or on the earth

beneath or in the waters below. You shall not bow down to them or worship them; for I, the Lord your God, am a jealous God, punishing the children for the sin of the parents to the third and fourth generation of those who hate me, but showing love to a thousand generations of those who love me and keep my commandments.

(Exodus 20:3-6, NIV)

This first commandment sets the right order to our loves. God, and only God, is to be our Lord. The second commandment, taking into consideration how creative He made humans to be, directs us to never create physical or spiritual idols. Stating that God is a jealous God drives home the point that He is to be our one and only Lord God. He promises us that He is the source of love to a thousand generations for those who have chosen to place Him first above all else and show our love by acting in harmony with His commandments.

The right order and placement of our love is simply stated more in Jesus' Greatest Commandments:

Jesus replied, "The most important commandment is this: 'Listen, O Israel! The Lord our God is the one and only Lord. And you must love the Lord your God with all your heart, all your soul, all your mind and with all your strength.' The second is equally important: 'Love your neighbor as yourself.' No other commandment is greater than these."

(Mark.12:29-31, NLT)

"Listen, O Israel!" Listening or hearing in the Hebrew language meant not only to hear but also to act upon what was heard. As in father-child relationship, God knows we hear Him only when we do what He says to do. God knows we may hear, but will we act upon what we in faith know? If not, what is holding us back?

God and Satan both know that the way we choose to order and place our love is critical to our spiritual growth, to our relevance, and to our enlightened influence in this dark and broken world. As subjects in the Kingdom of God on earth, we cannot play both sides. We cannot have two masters:

> "No servant is able to serve two masters; for either
> he will hate the one and love the other, or he will
> stand by and be devoted to the one and despise the
> other. You cannot serve God and mammon [riches,
> or anything in which you trust and on which you
> rely]."
> (Luke 16:13, AMP; also Matthew 6:24)

Once believers are justified by grace through faith, the Church and its team members enter into the sanctifying-faith process of becoming Christ-like and gaining His wisdom. In this sanctification character-building process, our love will be refined under fire and tested by the Word and Spirit of God in us. We are also held to account by the Family of God, God's team.

The Three Spiritual Battle Fronts

In his *Handbook to Spiritual Growth*, Ken Boa describes three spiritual battle fronts: our flesh, the world, and Satan. These spiritual battle fronts attempt to displace our loves and create idols. The deception of idols and gods is that they begin as something good. God created everything and called it "very good" (Genesis 1:31). Yet, we humans can quickly take what is good and make an idol of it. When we choose to idolize the created instead of the Creator, our chosen love object becomes an idol: it is evil and causes harm. This is spiritual warfare.

> For our struggle is not against human opponents, but against rulers, authorities, cosmic powers in the darkness around us, and evil spiritual forces in the heavenly realms.
> (Ephesians 6:12, ISV)

The Three Temptations of Jesus

Just as Jesus was tempted, we will be constantly tempted by the Tempter as we follow Jesus. Believers must learn to rely on the guidance of God's Word and the power of the indwelling Holy Spirit. In the first temptation, "Jesus was led by the Spirit into the desert to be tempted by the devil" (Matthew 4:1). Being Spirit-led, Jesus took the offensive against the enemy and settled His goodness. Jesus fasted for forty days and was very hungry. He was in this extremely weakened physical state when Satan attacked. So, where did the devil first attack Jesus, but the flesh? Satan told him, "If you are the Son of God, tell these stones to turn to bread"

76

(Matthew 4:3, NIV). Satan was tempting Jesus to use His powers and position to meet His own flesh, or physical needs of extreme hunger. Making bread would have shown that Jesus had not quite set aside all His power and position, had not humbled Himself, and had not identified completely with the human condition. Jesus, led by the Spirit, answered with the Sword of the Spirit, the Word of God (Deuteronomy 8:3). The devil's second temptation was taking Jesus to the highest point of the temple and saying "If you are the son of God, throw yourself down. For it is written: He will command His angels concerning you, and they will lift you up in their hands, so that you will not strike your foot against a stone" (Matthew 4:6, NIV). As Satan quoted Scripture (Psalms 91:11-12) out of context, he wanted Jesus to question His relationship with His Father by testing His Father's character and Word for faithfulness and truthfulness with a ridiculous act that was outside of God's Will, and a sin. Here Satan shows that he will attack our relationship with God by creating doubt in our minds by contorting Scripture, especially when we are vulnerable and weak, and will attempt to provide a worldly context to our thinking. Knowing Scripture and recognizing that Satan himself was wrongly using it, Jesus aggressively responded again with Scripture (Deuteronomy. 6:16). In the third temptation, Satan takes Jesus to the highest mountains and shows Him all the kingdoms of the world and says, "All this I will give you, if you will bow down and worship me" (Matthew 4:9, NIV). Satan tempted Jesus, the King, to take the world as an earthly kingdom, without carrying out God's plan of salvation through the pain of the cross. Satan tempted Jesus to take the easy way out. Yet, Satan's supreme desire was for Jesus (and all peoples) to bow down to him and none other. Satan wanted to own Jesus' heart, as he wants to own our hearts. Satan desires us to settle for less by worshipping him above all else with all of our minds, hearts, bodies, and souls. As Satan tempted Jesus with worldly wealth and power, Satan does the same with us. Again, quoting Scripture (Deuteronomy 6:13) Jesus replied, "Away from me, Satan! For it is written: 'Worship the Lord your God, and serve Him only'" (Matthew 4:10). Obeying Jesus, Satan left.

> Jesus says, "The thief does not come except to steal, and to kill, and to destroy. I have come that they may have life, and that they may have it more abundantly."
> (John 10:10, NKJV)

In this cosmic battle for the heart of mankind, Christ Followers, individually and collectively, must always remain centered in both the Spirit and Word of God, while knowing that Satan will attack on all three battle fronts—the flesh, the world, and Satan himself.

The Four Soils of the Human Heart

In Matthew 13:1-23, Mark 4:1-20, and Luke 8:1-13, Jesus teaches receptive people in parable form about the Four Soils of people's heart. The attitude and condition of their hearts will govern their response. This parable was covered in detail in Book 1, Chapter 3, but it is worth reviewing here:

1) The first type of soil is where the Sower's seeds (Word of God) fall on the hard, well-compacted soil of a foot-path or road. These seeds are

unable to take root, and the birds (Satan) quickly take away these seeds. These seeds planted in hard hearts never have a chance to grow due to a person's non-receptive response. These hearts are hardened, and the Good News Word of God cannot take root in hearts of stone.

2) The second soil reflects the seeds that fall on the shallow top soil lying above rocks and gravel. These seeds are received joyfully and understand some Good News basics, but due to shallowness, they are unable to allow God's truth to work its way deeper in their hearts and make a difference in their lives. They have shallow roots and die quickly in times of drought and trouble. The shallow soil reflects an undeveloped character that is usually led by an emotional response to the Word. Yet Satan uses our sorrow, pain, trouble, and even persecution to draw the "shallow believers" away from God and unto himself. As a result, they will fall away from the Word quickly.

3) The third soil reflects the seeds that fall among the thicket and thorns. Satan's worldly thickets, weeds, and thorns rob the seeds of nourishment and hinder their growth and production. We grow up in this environment that the world has normalized. This type of soil yields the very "thickets" that drag us down, hold us back, and impede our growth. The Word is crowded out by our worldly cares and worries. The Word is choked off by individualism, materialism, and

ethnocentrism, or cultural idolatry; no crop is produced.

4) There is a fourth good soil that has been nurtured and faithfully worked. It reflects hearts of flesh that have been willingly transformed and regenerated by the Word of God and the Spirit of God within the Family of God and trained up to do and abide in the Will of God. It comes forth through our faithful agape love for God and others. This heart of flesh is promised to produce a hundred-fold a "love that never fails" (1 Corinthians 13:8). Nothing is able to hold these free and empowered hearts back.

In reviewing the Three Temptations of Jesus and the Four Soils of the Human Heart, we note that Satan is competing to be the center of our world and our flesh. These battle fronts are where the devil is prowling and planning his constant attacks. Our defense and offense are established in developing the good soil, the fourth soil, where the Seed can establish its unseen deep, strong, healthy root system that promises to produce our Lord's character.

Preparatory Prayer and Action

Pastors sometimes say that motivating folks to get up off their pews and engage in life is one of their major struggles, and if we are honest, it is a major problem with us all. When we do act, we seem to act for action's sake. Yet, repetitive actions that don't have a growing, strong, holistic theology based in love and prayerful reflection often cause harm in the name of good.

In the Mary and Martha story (Luke 10:38-42), Martha does a good thing by opening her home to Jesus. Both Mary and Martha loved Jesus, and both were serving Him. Mary was sitting and listening at Jesus' feet, but Martha thought her own actions were more important. Many times, without prayerful meditations, we allow our actions to become self-serving, as happened with Martha. Both prayer and actions together are good and needed, yet Jesus does say one is better. Let us not degenerate into the ditch of busy work that no longer has our Christ-focused devotion, and let us not fall into the other ditch of a monk-ism that removes us from being engaged in life all together. Both prayer and action are designed to go together, and each requires the other.

The necessity of both prayer and actions is why Paul gives us the theology first and the practical application second in his New Testament letters. To avoid causing further harm we must, according to God's revealed Will, have our loves in the right place and order before our actions begin, or we will be bad witnesses. And in the Spirit, our actions must always be balanced with our quiet meditative time in God's word at Christ's feet. Being led by both the Word and Spirit, our prayerful reflections will drive us into action, and our actions will drive us back into prayer. These repetitive cycles will drill us deeper and deeper into our relationships with God and neighbors while training us up in Christ-likeness.

THE "*PRAYER-ACTION*" CYCLE

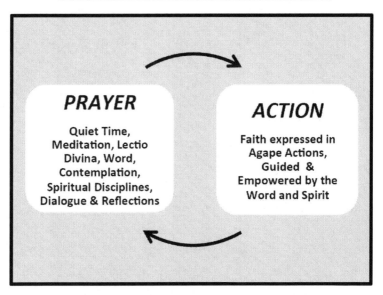

PRAYER

Quiet Time,
Meditation, Lectio
Divina, Word,
Contemplation,
Spiritual Disciplines,
Dialogue & Reflections

ACTION

Faith expressed in
Agape Actions,
Guided &
Empowered by the
Word and Spirit

**Loving Action Requires Empowering Prayer,
Empowering Prayer Requires Loving Action**

**"The more humble one is at God's feet,
The more useful he is at God's hand"
(Watchman Nee)**

Winning the Battle

Many American Christians generally understand the message of salvation, but often struggle to understand the "carry your cross" daily message (cost of discipleship). Yet, the agape love process of letting go and dying-to-self is our initial conversion step in the sanctifying-faith process. In many instances, we come to Christ when the pain of holding on simply outweighs the fear of letting go. Upon letting go, there becomes less of "me" and more of God, and we begin the process of slowly dying to self ("Whoever loves his life loses it" John 12:25a, ESV). This initial conversion, the dying-to-self process of agape love, now sets the pattern for our continued spiritual training and growth in becoming more and more Christ-like in character. Our conversion moment is the first step of many towards dying to our false self. The Way of agape love is the guts of God's character training and tough-love process.

> "Then he said to them all: 'Whoever wants to be my disciple must deny themselves and take up their cross daily and follow me.'"
> (Luke 9:23, AMP)

> Therefore, I urge you, brothers and sisters, in view of God's mercy, to offer your bodies as a living sacrifice, holy and pleasing to God—this is your true and proper worship.
> (Romans 12:1, NIV)

For more information on the cost of being a disciple, see Luke 14:25-35.

In America today, the family is under severe attack. Broken relationships, single parent homes and illegitimacy often result in poverty and wound our children and neighborhoods deeply. Our family breakups are due to our failed battles with the flesh, worldly enticements, and Satan. Without Christ's character-development training in us, we are defenseless against these attacks.

After all, it is Christ's character being developed in obedient followers through agape love that will deliver victory over the flesh, the world, and Satan.

> The Great Guide, Identifier, Transformer, and Empowerer is Agape Love.

Idolatry

As Christianity embraces the Holy Trinity, our American culture embraces its own Holy Trinity too, which might be better stated as being our Unholy Trinity:

1) Materialism (loving, trusting and relying on money, and other material things, before God; material-centered);
2) Individualism (includes selfishness, self-indulgences, addictions, pride, foolishness, self-centered);
3) Ethnocentrism (group superiority, racism, dualistic thought, group-centered.

It may be noted that there are hundreds of idols and addictions that can be listed under one or more of these three categories. America's Unholy Trinity has produced a culture of "-holics" and "-isms" of one type or another which have been culturally normalized. And we wonder why we "stumble in the dark."

Each of America's Unholy Trinity has its own temple of worship. At each temple there are sacrifices. In the Temple of Materialism, we sacrifice God. We trust and love material things and rely on them and not our one and only Lord God. In the Temple of Individualism, we sacrifice our true self by not acquiring the wisdom that is gained by wholeheartedly loving God and others. We become foolish in what we think, say, and do. In our foolishness, we do not rightly love ourselves (Proverbs 19:8a, NLT). In the Temple of Ethnocentrism, we sacrifice our neighbors who are not like us. We become dualistic in our thinking. Our ingrown group believes it is right and all other groups are wrong. Our group says, "We are 'in,' and they are 'out.'" It may be noted that many of our hundreds of idols ("-isms" and "-holics") demand us to worship at more than just one of these unholy temples where we sacrifice the grace and truth of Christ Jesus. America's Unholy Trinity is our world's unholy worship to which Christians are called to not conform.

> Do not be conformed to this world, but
> continuously be transformed by the renewing of
> your minds so that you may be able to determine
> what God's will is – what is proper, pleasing and
> perfect.
> (Romans 12:2, ISV)

> Do not love the world.
> (1 John 2:15, NIV)

Our displaced loves (idolatry, gods) rooted in the flesh and the world will hold us back and divide us spiritually while we fear letting go of them.

Jesus's antidote to America's Unholy Trinity is to choose to love and give place to what God loves and directs us to love:

85

1) Loving God (not giving place to material-centeredness);
2) Loving ourselves by acquiring wisdom (not giving place to foolish self-centeredness);
3) Loving our neighbor who isn't like us (not giving place to inbred group-centeredness).

Thus, the great antidote to idolatry is Jesus' Greatest Commandments. And our Lord promises us that "Love never fails" (1 Corinthians 13:8).

As with all idols, demolishing these false gods begins with:

1) Admitting our idolatry and helplessness without our Lord and King;
2) Committing ourselves to choosing to place God and others first;
3) Submitting ourselves to thrive and live under our King's loving rule, all the while being in the family of God that is faithfully guided by the Word of God and empowered by the indwelling Spirit of God.

Nelson:

In trying to understand "idols" and "gods," I have spent a year reading and reflecting on Old and New Testament Scripture. I have asked God to reveal to me how He views cultural and individual idols and gods. As always, I read scripture through the lens of the Greatest Commandments keeping my questions and burdens uppermost in my mind, watching the Spirit connect the dots, and training myself to see these idols. I bought a 365 Day Bible and carried this question in my heart and mind for that year's reading. If you like this process, ask a group of your friends to join you and meet weekly to discuss how God is speaking to you through His Spirit and Word. Mark up your 365 Day Bible, making many notes, and plan someday to gift your marked-up 365 Day Bible to your children.

What about Satan? We must always "Be alert and of sober mind. Your enemy the devil prowls around like a roaring lion looking for someone to devour" (1 Peter 5:8, NIV). That "someone to devour" is you, your spouse, your children, family, church family, and the larger church family, your extended family, friends, co-workers, business, city, community, state, nation and beyond—all meaning you and your neighbors. The battle is real, the fight is between light and darkness, and it is for your heart.

Do a Bible Word Search online, and meditate on God's warnings to be careful, be on guard, watch out, don't forget, remember, and don't turn left or right.

Praise to God and the Father of our Lord Jesus Christ! Being united in Christ we are now fully blessed with every spiritual blessing that heaven has to offer (paraphrased from Ephesians 1:3, NLT and GW). Our Lord will not send us into battle untrained and unequipped. In being lovingly united and crowned in Christ's Spirit and guided by His law of love, we are to be fully trained and equipped as needed to wisely discern and fight the spiritual battles on all three fronts, while knowing fully that Christ's victory is ultimately ours, that death does not have the last word, and that there is hope. Let us put on the Armor of God and never take it off.

QUESTIONS

1. What product is our Christian culture (system) producing?

2. What changes to the system are needed to produce Christ-like followers?

3. Why is God so concerned about idols and idolatry?

4. The battle fronts are the flesh, the world, and Satan. Satan tempted Jesus with food/hunger (flesh); power (the world); and making himself (Satan) king. He tempts us with the same thing. Is any one of these three more troublesome to you than the others? Explain.

5. The seed that fell on the rocky soil and had no root for difficult times represents both the flesh and devil. The seed sown among thorns represents the flesh and the world. How strong and complete is your walk with Jesus today? Do you see any similar weaknesses in your life today that God desires to strengthen?

6. Do you see yourself in any aspect of your life as a materialist? Or as an individualist? Or as an ethno centrist? Where do you need the Holy Spirit to begin His work to help you deal with this idol? What is the antidote against these three idols?

CHAPTER FIVE

The Armor of God

Why Is Christ-Like Character Development So Important?

The character of both the King and Kingdom have been Biblically described as being full of Grace (Salvation and Spirit)—Faith in the Truth—Love—Righteousness—Justice—Shalom. K2 explores how these characteristics also relate to the Armor of God.

Why Are We to Put on the Armor of God?

Scripture tells us, "Stay alert! Watch out for your great enemy, the devil. He prowls around like a roaring lion, looking for someone to devour." (1 Peter 5:8, NLT)

Peter warns us to stay alert and watch out. Yes, we can cast all our cares on God (1 Peter 5:7), but we must also be careful, on guard, and ever alert for God's enemy, the devil, and his constant workings around us everywhere. All affliction and persecution facing believers ultimately comes down to this one source, the devil, also known as Satan, Accuser, Tempter, Liar, Beelzebub. Satan is the source of all evil in the world and constantly prowls around looking for opportunity to attack. Satan hates God, God's family, and all families and has declared war on them. Ours is a spiritual battle where Satan is constantly fighting for the premier affections of our hearts. "Put on all of God's armor":

> A final word: Be strong in the Lord and in his mighty power. Put on all of God's armor so that you will be able to stand firm against all strategies of the devil. For we are not fighting against flesh-and-blood enemies, but against evil rulers and authorities of the unseen world, against mighty powers in this dark world, and against evil spirits in the heavenly places. Therefore, put on every piece of God's armor so you will be able to resist the enemy in the time of evil. Then after the battle you will still be standing firm.
> (Ephesians 6:10-13, NLT)

Everyone is familiar with the story of David and Goliath (1 Samuel 17:1-52). Goliath was a nine-foot tall giant covered with impenetrable armor and carrying weapons that no man was able to withstand. None of the Israelite soldiers, even protected by their own armor and weapons felt capable of defeating this giant. Fear gripped them all. On the other hand, David was a seventeen-year-old shepherd of average size who owned no armor or weapons of war. When King Saul accepted David's offer to fight Goliath, he did as any soldier facing a worldly enemy would do and offered his armor and sword to David, but David rejected the offer. Even though the fight was between two men, David saw that this was actually a spiritual battle. Using a sling and stones as his only weapon, "David said to the Philistine, 'You come against me with sword and spear and javelin, but I come against you in the name of the Lord Almighty, the God of the armies of Israel, whom you have defied. This day the Lord will hand you over to me, and I'll strike you down and cut off your head. Today I will give the carcasses of the Philistine army to the birds of the air and the beasts of the earth, and the whole world will know that there is a God in Israel'. All those gathered here will know that it is not by sword or spear that the Lord saves; for the battle is the Lord's and He will give all of you into our hands" (1 Samuel 17:1-52, NIV).

Worldly weapons have no effect in spiritual warfare. We have to recognize the warfare for what it truly is, "For we are not fighting against flesh-and-blood enemies." Our Christian path is to choose to follow God and rely on His provision.

In our lives, there is a fork in the road where one road has a narrow gate and is less traveled, while the other road has a wide gate and is well-traveled. Which road to choose? The Word of God directs us to "enter through the narrow gate. For wide is the gate and broad is the road that leads to destruction. But small is the gate and narrow the road that leads to life, and only a few find it" (Matthew 7:13-14, NIV).

Satan's wide road lures us by appealing to our earthly desires. Satan promises us our heart's deepest desire, our God-given desire for heaven on earth, but his promises can never deliver that which he does not possess. At first, his promises are sweet to lure people in, but they quickly turn into bitter lies.

Satan's promises also fall short for a number of reasons: Satan despises the truth (John 8:44); Satan masquerades as an angel of light (2 Corinthians 11:14-15); Satan steals, kills, and destroys (John 10:10); Satan rules the masses outside of God's protection (Ephesians 2:1-3); Satan prowls around looking for opportunities (Luke 4:13); Satan hides the truth (2 Corinthians 4:3-4); Satan offers counterfeit promises (Genesis 3:4-5); Satan twists scripture (Genesis 3:1-5). When we, as Christ followers, know Jesus and compare what He says and how He says it with Satan's way, we ought to be able to distinguish who it is that is speaking to us. But in the end Satan will suffer his fate (Revelations 20:10).

Christ Jesus' narrow gate is the entrance to God's caring, right, and true path that becomes sweeter and sweeter in time. Christ Jesus describes Himself as this narrow gate that leads to true life.

Jesus says, "Yes, I am the gate . . ." (John 10:9, NLT).

Jesus answered, "I am the way and the truth and the life" (John 14:6a, NIV).

Faithfully entering Jesus's narrow and righteous gateway promises to deliver the full measure of our deepest human desires "on earth as it is in heaven." Christ's narrow path also promises to shine brighter and clearer as we walk along it, as opposed to the dark path.

> But the path of the just (righteous) is like the light of dawn, That shines brighter and brighter until [it reaches its full strength and glory in] the perfect day.

The way of the wicked is like [deep] darkness; They
do not know over what they stumble.
(Proverbs 4:18-19, AMP)

After entering through Jesus' gate, we are told to put on the
Armor of God. Paul writes "Put on all of God's
armor." "Put on," from the Greek word *enduo*, carries the
idea of permanence. The full Armor of God is not something
to be put on and taken off occasionally, but is something to
be put on permanently. It is Christ's character we are to put
on. It is who we are becoming.

> Therefore, put on every piece of God's armor so
> you will be able to resist the enemy in the time of
> evil. Then after the battle you will still be standing
> firm. Stand your ground, putting on the belt of truth
> and the body armor of God's righteousness. For
> shoes, put on the peace that comes from the Good
> News so that you will be fully prepared. In addition
> to all of these, hold up the shield of faith to stop the
> fiery arrows of the devil. Put on salvation as your
> helmet, and take the sword of the Spirit, which is
> the word of God. Pray in the Spirit at all times and
> on every occasion. Stay alert and be persistent in
> your prayers for all believers everywhere. And pray
> for me, too. Ask God to give me the right words so
> I can boldly explain God's mysterious plan that the
> Good News is for Jews and Gentiles alike. I am in
> chains now, still preaching this message as God's
> ambassador. So pray that I will keep on speaking
> boldly for him, as I should.
> (Ephesians 6:13-20, NLT)

Ephesians 6:13-20 tells the characteristics of this armor:

- Grace (New Covenant Grace of Salvation and Spirit)
- Faith (in the Truth)
- Truth (Christ Jesus)
- Righteousness (and justice)
- Peace (shalom)
- Pray in the Spirit of God (quiet time, meditation)

What about love? Put on the armor of love:

> But let us who live in the light be clearheaded, protected by the armor of faith and love, and wearing as our helmet the confidence of our salvation.
> (1 Thessalonians 5:8, NLT)

Paul points out that agape love is the most important part of God's armor for the Christian soldier. Paul also writes that believers are empty and are nothing without love:

> And if I have prophetic powers [the gift of interpreting the divine will and purpose], and understand all the secret truths and mysteries and possess all knowledge, and if I have [sufficient] faith so that I can remove mountains, but have not love [God's love in me] I am nothing [a useless nobody]."
> (1 Corinthians 13:2, AMP)

And our Shield of Faith (Ephesians 6:16) anchored in the truth of Christ Jesus must be expressed in agape love: "The only thing that counts is faith expressing itself in love" (Galatians 5:6b, NIV).

Like an overcoat, "put on love":

> And over all these virtues put on love, which binds
> them all together in perfect unity.
> (Colossians 3:14, NIV)

And God promises us that love is life's toughest stuff which never comes to an end or fails.

> Love never fails.
> (1 Corinthians 13:8, NIV)

Living a life centered in Christ, in both His Word and Spirit, is the key to the love that never fails. So, through agape love, let's put on the full armor of light, the character of Christ.

> The night is advanced, the day is at hand. Let us
> then throw off the works of darkness [and] put on
> the armor of light...put on the Lord Jesus Christ,
> and make no provision for the desires of the flesh.
> (Romans 13:12, 14, NABRE)

The Light in us is our new reality. Jesus said, "I am the Light of the world; he who follows Me will not walk in darkness, but will have the Light of life" (John 8:12, NASB).

Biblically compare the description of the Armor of God with the Character of the King and Kingdom. The Armor of God is comprised of the same characteristics as both the King and the Kingdom of God. "Putting on" the full Armor of God is "putting on" Christ's character! This is prayerfully and obediently done by our daily exercising and habitual training within Jesus' Greatest Commandments, His will. God's purpose for His family is to conform us to His Son's image and character (Romans 8:28-29). In growing up in the character of the King and Kingdom, we will not only be equipped to fend off satanic attacks, but also to discover our true identity, meaning, and purpose in life. As Christ develops His character and wisdom in believers, we will be more fully enlightened to understand God's initial and primary desire to fully develop His image and likeness in all of mankind (Genesis 1:26-27).

God's vision for us is to develop the right and loving habits that lead to becoming more and more Christ-like in character, which is the Armor of God that is to never come off. It is who we truly are. Our character development occurs within the framework of the will of God's Greatest Commandments of agape love. It is God's "Agape Process." It is important for us to constantly meditate on and actively practice these refining character habits. Over the years, we meditate and act in both the Word and Spirit on each piece of the armor of God, the character of God, and the Kingdom of God, as we learn to wisely apply each piece of the King's character in every aspect of our lives. Christ, being our center, is the key to His most important character trait of love. Submitting and committing ourselves to our King's rule is for the betterment of ourselves and the Kingdom of God on earth as it is in heaven.

The Armor of God is the King and the Kingdom's character traits that are the high standards to which believers are to aim and attain. Shedding the foolishness and lies of Satan by acquiring the loving truths of our Lord, believers begin gaining the wisdom of Christ in becoming like Him. Putting on the Armor of God is putting on Christ's powerful character and wisdom.

> Christ is the power of God and the wisdom of God.
> (1 Corinthians 1:24b, AMP)

In acquiring God's wisdom, we are rightly loving ourselves. "To acquire wisdom is to love yourself" (Proverbs 19:8a, NLT). The root issue in most secular and worldly problems comes down to people not liking themselves very much. Up front, this seems to be an odd statement and something that may be hard to discern. But whenever people seek foolishness, instead of acquiring the character of Christ, they are not biblically loving themselves. Only in Christ can a person wisely discern such things.

God arms and equips believers for His good battle. While most of God's armor appears defensive in nature—belt, armor, shoes, shield, helmet—the one offensive weapon is "the sword of the Spirit, which is the Word of God" that directs us to go inflict love on the world where we are. Practice employing each weapon for its intended purpose, whenever and wherever necessary. In addition, never forget, the Body of Christ is further equipped with every spiritual gift.

> May blessing [praise, laudation, and eulogy] be to the God and Father of our Lord Jesus Christ [the Messiah] Who has blessed us in Christ with every spiritual [given by the Holy Spirit] blessing in the heavenly realm!
> (Ephesians 1:3, AMP)

Yet God wages this war of love much differently than the secular world fights for our love. The world's weapons of selfish indulgences, materialism, ethnocentrism, political power, pride, prestige, comforts, and conveniences pander to our human flesh, to the world, and to Satan's desire for our allegiance and love.

> We are human, but we don't wage war as humans do. We use God's mighty weapons, not worldly weapons, to knock down the strongholds of human reasoning and to destroy false arguments.
> (2 Corinthians 10:3-4, NLT)

God's Battle Plan Is Agape Love

God's plan for this spiritual warfare is done within the revealed Will of God as given to us in the Word of God:

> Jesus replied, "'You must love the Lord your God with all your heart, all your soul, and all your mind.' This is the first and greatest commandment. A second is equally important: 'Love your neighbor as yourself.' The entire law and all the demands of the prophets are based on these two commandments."
> (Matthew 22:37-40, NLT)

We are enabled to love at the "no harm" level of agape love when we are graciously clothed with the presence of Christ Jesus' Spirit, obediently living in the light of God, and empowered to not indulge our fleshly desires or conform to the world.

[Agape] Love does no wrong to others, so love fulfills the requirements of God's law…The night is almost gone; the day of salvation will soon be here. So remove your dark deeds like dirty clothes, and put on the shining armor of right living…clothe yourself with the presence of the Lord Jesus Christ. And don't let yourself think about ways to indulge your evil desires.
(Romans 13:10, 12, 14 NLT)

> The full Armor of God is the Character of the King and Kingdom on earth and His Wisdom: Full of Grace (Salvation and Spirit), Faith (anchored in the Truth of Christ Jesus), Agape Love, Righteousness, Justice, and Shalom (peace, joy and wholeness).

Each piece of armor represents Christ's character. Learning and experiencing how to apply these pieces and habitually using them develops the full character and wisdom of Christ in our lives and that of His Church Body. The indwelling Word of God and the Spirit of God, when obediently and habitually followed, will develop Christ's character in us, so we will live the whole life that God wants for us, while also destroying the devil's work. This is God's revealed system that produces the product of His character.

What is the best way to put on the Armor of God, God's character? Christ's character, the Armor of God, is best developed by loving God and self and boldly choosing to enter the heart-felt pain of Christ by intentionally choosing to love our neighbors who are not like ourselves, our Samaritans.

> If you love those who love you, what benefit is that
> to you? For even sinners love those who love them.
> (Luke 6:32, ESV)

Why put on the Armor of God? We put on the full Armor of God, the character of God, by becoming more like the One we have chosen to love, Jesus Christ, our King. We, the Church Body, become more and more Christ-like in character as we choose to love what God loves. We put on the full Armor of God (Christ Character and Wisdom) for the sake of peace (wholeness, shalom) in our King's Kingdom on earth as it is in heaven. We put on the Armor of God for love and His glory! We put on the armor of God to lift burdens and close gaps around us. We also put on the Armor of God to better see our true selves as originally created. We put on the Armor of God to fight, defend ourselves, and destroy the devil's work that is constantly trying to hold humanity down and even kill people. So, we do what Christ came to do.

> The reason the Son of God appeared was to destroy
> the devil's work.
> (1 John 3:8b, NIV)

The whole Armor of God is our defense and offense that protects and destroys Satan's desires to occupy and dominate our minds, hearts, and actions. Christ Character, which permeates the Kingdom and His Family, is the antidote for all Christians who are attacked and held back from living and maturing in the Christian walk. Habitually abiding in God's will (the Greatest Commandments, His system) develops Christ-like character (His system's product or goal) in His followers. The product God desires to create through His Agape Love Teaching-Training System is Christ-like character in us, individually and collectively. By putting on the armor of God or developing the character of Christ Jesus, Christians are further able to wisely see and experience their original true identity as beings created in the image and likeness of God (Genesis 1:26-27). Then our King's Kingdom can come and His will be done on earth as it is in heaven for God's glory.

> God the Father sent His Son. His Son sent His Spirit. His Spirit sends the Church (large "C").
>
> "As you sent me into the world, I have sent them into the world." (John 17:18, NIV)
>
> Jesus said, "Peace be with you! As the Father has sent me, I am sending you." (John 20:21, NIV)

God's Promise:

> And the God of peace will soon crush Satan under your feet. The grace of our Lord Jesus Christ [the Messiah] be with you.
> (Romans 16:20, AMP)

> You, dear children, are from God and have overcome them, because the one who is in you is greater than the one who is in the world.
> (1 John 4:4, NIV)

Upon this rock I will build my Church, and all the powers of hell will not conquer it.
(Matthew 16:18, NLT)

As we become more and more like our Savior and Lord, we learn to place our wholehearted confidence on the Rock of who He says He is and what He promises those of us who believe. In placing all confidence on our Lord Jesus Christ, we enter into His rest and joy.

QUESTIONS

1. What is the narrow path?

2. Why is it narrow and why do few find it?

3. Why is the wide road so well-traveled?

4. Every piece of God's armor is equally important, the same as every aspect of God's revealed character. What are some of the ways we can develop God's characteristics and properly apply pieces of God's armor?

5. Describe the Spirit-filled loving process in building Christ-like character in us (refer to Romans 5:1-5).

6. When you hear condemning words in your mind (conscience), do you immediately recognize that this is not Jesus speaking to you? (Romans 8:1)

CHAPTER SIX

The Joy of God

Joy is the settled assurance that God is in control of all the details of my life, the quiet confidence that ultimately everything is going to be alright, and the determined choice to praise God in every situation. (Rick Warren)

I slept and dreamt that life was joy. I awoke and saw that life was service. I acted and behold, service was joy.
(Rabindranath Tagore)

Through experience, Kelle Oliphint's motto became "Service is Joy."

What does the Bible say about the ideas of joy and fun? God intends for you to have fun. How do we know that? Psalm 23:5 says, "He will set a table for you in the presence of your enemies." Your job is to have fun and enjoy. By the way, if you're not having fun, you're not in the will of God, or you haven't experienced the fullness of His joy.

The book of John is full of Jesus saying: "I want you to have My joy—and to its fullest." It's something you can have now. It's something He paid for on the cross. Jesus desires his disciples' joy to be complete (John 15:11). You may be saying, "But I do not feel God's joy!" The book of Haggai basically says that if you're sowing much and reaping little, consider your ways:

> You have planted much, but harvested little. You eat, but never have enough. You drink, but never have your fill. You put on clothes, but are not warm. You earn wages, only to put them in a purse with holes in it. This is what the Lord Almighty says: "Give careful thought to your ways."
> (Haggai 1:6-7, NIV)

Your job is to have joy. Otherwise joy wouldn't be in the list of the Fruits of the Spirit. Notice it's the second one. If you look at the Fruits of the Spirit: love, joy, peace, patience, kindness, goodness, faithfulness, self-control (Galatians 5:22-23), you see they grow in that particular order. If you don't have agape love, you can't have joy. If you don't have joy, you can't have peace. If you don't have peace, you can't have patience. So if you're feeling impatient, it's connected to something else in your life. You're not loving. You're not full of joy. By the way, if your problem is with self-control, it's not so much about self-control; it's all the preceding stuff.

The basic truth about it is the word "love" is the Hebrew word *hesed*, which means "in all things I choose you first." *Hesed* is a choice—not an emotion. The emotional love comes after you choose to love consistently. The emotion of joy comes after you choose joy consistently. By the way, the word "joy" means "that which I have confidence in." It's not happy glee; it's what I put my confidence in. So when you hear "the joy of the Lord is my strength," it means the confidence I put in the Lord is my strength. So if you love God and love what He loves, and you put your confidence in Him, then you have a right to hold Him to our Father's promise that nothing is missing or broken (shalom) in your life. Confidence in the character of God and confidence in what He said He would do is joy.

God sent his word. Why? So that you could bring the Kingdom of God here. But you might say, "I don't know if I believe that." Great. That ain't God, that ain't the Holy Spirit, that ain't anybody but you. Why? Because you're not sure, you're not settled in your confidence.

So in all things I have the confidence in God, in His character and capability of getting a thing done—that's joy. You know what the opposing force is? I have confidence in me and my ability to deliver on promises. That's pride. We have all tried to be God, but we are not qualified. You know when I get in trouble? I put my confidence in me when I try to help Him.

So how do you bring joy? Psalm 16:11 (NKJV) says, "…In Your presence is fullness of joy…" First, how do you develop joy? You constantly put yourself in the presence of God and expect him to do what He said. That is not arrogance. That is confidence in God! Practice the presence of God in everything you do. Practice our Father's presence because in the presence of God is fullness of joy.

Psalm 22:3 says that God inhabits the praises of His people. "But thou art holy, O thou that inhabitest the praises of Israel" (KJV). So how do you practice the presence of

God? First you praise Him. Start your day and fill it with praise constantly. Praise! Matter of fact, if you get in an ugly situation, start with praise.

Jeremiah 15:16 (NKJV) says: "...Your word was to me the joy and rejoicing of my heart," meaning both praise and the Word—filling your head and your mouth and your heart with the Word of God. What does that do? Well, Isaiah 61:3 says that the oil of joy is your confidence for mourning. So what happens next is the anointing of the Holy Spirit.

So, again, how do I develop joy? Well, first I should fill my mouth with praise constantly. When I'm driving, instead of cursing at that person who cut me off, I ought to praise God for that, because apparently there's some reason they're slowing me down. Maybe if I was a little bit faster, I'd get killed by a truck. I don't know what it is. But what I can tell you is if you look for the praise in it, what will happen is you'll start to laugh.

It's the anointing that does the work. Read Genesis 1. Who created light? Everybody says God. No, it was the Holy Spirit that created light. God said light, the Holy Spirit brought it, and God said that it was good. To use it in a business sense, the capital, the cash with God, is the anointing. It's the thing that pays the bill. And it always follows the Word, spoken in faith. So, if you've got the presence of God and you're studying the Word of God, the anointing comes to deliver whatever you're reading. So where is your strength? It's in the Word of God delivered by the anointing of the Spirit.

So, how do we develop joy? First, we start with praise. Next we look at the Word of God, and then we expect the Holy Spirit to come around the Word of God. Whatever it says, we have a right to expect. Have you ever heard somebody say "press God"? Here's an example.

Tom:

> So I had this niece and nephew who came to visit us years ago when we were living in Shreveport. We got up, and we were sitting there at breakfast and having a nice conversation, and Robert and Catherine said, you know, Uncle Tom, I'd really like to have a hamburger from McDonald's tonight.
>
> I said, great. Later that evening we're sitting there eating dinner, and they're frowning. I said, what's the matter?
>
> They said, I thought we were going to McDonald's.
>
> I went, oh. Okay, tomorrow.
>
> So I got to work; I get to work every morning at least by seven o'clock. About 7:30 the phone rings, and it's Catherine, and she says, Uncle Tom, I want to thank you for taking me to McDonald's tonight. Okay, Catherine.
>
> About 10 o'clock the phone rings, it's Robert. He says, Uncle Tom, I'm so excited about McDonald's. This occurred eight or ten times during the day.
>
> Let me tell you something. The Scripture says, put God in remembrance of his Word, but if you add it as praise and thanksgiving, it's astounding the joy that comes.
>
> I had expectation all day long of getting them a hamburger. And it was just a hamburger. Imagine if you apply it to work or healing or your life or peace of mind, or whatever it is. The Word of God is

already written to give you a guarantee, and all you do is find it and get excited about it and say, Lord, I cannot wait to see what you're going to do.

And then, by the way, when ugly shows up, you still have confidence in God. Because let me tell you the fourth part. The day you make your stand on that confidence, the devil immediately will begin to attack you, because you are a dangerous thing to him. So oddly enough, one of the indicators of being on the right path is that an attack comes. If everything is calm and peaceful, you're missing something.

To summarize, you need to understand that first there's praise, then there's Word, and then there's the Holy Spirit, but there is a commitment and an expectation built into the whole process. We firmly believe that God has better thoughts than we do and has better plans than we have. And we willingly and lovingly place our trust in those thoughts and plans. Jesus said (paraphrasing John 15:11):

> I say these things, these words, these covenant words to you so that my joy will be in you and that my joy will be full. I say these things to you so your confidence in God and his way of doing things will be in you just like it's in me, so that my joy will be full in you.

Jeremiah 29:11 starts this way, and it's written in the original Hebrew this way: "The plans I have for you..." To the Hebrew ears, God is brimming with joy for mankind as He speaks through Jeremiah. "Oh, man. You ought to see what I have in store. I want to take you from captivity and put you on high." Listen to that energy. You see that joy?

"I am the true vine, and my Father is the gardener. He cuts off every branch in me that bears no fruit, while every branch that does bear fruit he prunes so that it will be even more fruitful. You are already clean because of the word I have spoken to you. Remain in me, as I also remain in you. No branch can bear fruit by itself; it must remain in the vine. Neither can you bear fruit unless you remain in me. I am the vine; you are the branches. If you remain in me and I in you, you will bear much fruit; apart from me you can do nothing. If you do not remain in me, you are like a branch that is thrown away and withers; such branches are picked up, thrown into the fire and burned. If you remain in me and my words remain in you, ask whatever you wish, and it will be done for you. This is to my Father's glory, that you bear much fruit, showing yourselves to be my disciples. As the Father has loved me, so have I loved you. Now remain in my love. If you keep my commands, you will remain in my love, just as I have kept my Father's commands and remain in his love. I have told you this so that my joy may be in you and that your joy may be complete."
(John 15:1-11, NIV)

This is the "Joy Process," and we will go through the steps very quickly, so you can study and embrace it on your own. Write the process out in your words, allowing them to drop from your head and into your heart. John 15:1-11 basically says, "I can do nothing of myself." When he says "nothing," he means nothing. So, if you want to know where joy comes from, it starts this way:

I've got nothing. Even if I think I've got something, I've got nothing. That's first. And by the way, just so we're on the same page, this idea can be really hard to accept. The next thing it says, you abide in me, and I abide in you. The Scripture says that if you love God, you abide in him. So first, it's to admit I can do nothing. The second thing is to say I'm going to faithfully commit to love God and love what God loves. Then the anointing and the glory come. The next thing is the Word comes, and then joy comes. It's in that order, and it's fun!

So, there's a process, but it starts with an odd premise: "I can do nothing!" Then I'm going to commit myself to faithfully loving God and loving what God loves. I'm going to commit to His Word day and night. The first item in the Word is this; I'm going to praise you for everything. I'm going to spend time; I'm going to start with praise and thanksgiving. Praise and thanks built into your life on a daily basis bring constant revelation, constant opportunities. Why? Because praise and thanks bring the presence of God.

So, what will my day look like? First: Lord, I faithfully commit to love You with all my heart, mind, soul, and spirit, and love what You love even if I don't like it. Next, I'm going to praise You; I'm going to thank You; I'm going to spend time with You; and I'm going to be in love with Your Word, because whatever You say in Your Word, You've already committed to do. So, there's praise, there's Word, there's the Holy Spirit, but your job then is to wait upon the Lord. What does that mean? That means once it's settled, your job is to be just like a waiter—Lord, what can I do for you today? Show up with a tray. It's not "wait," as in biding your time.

I discovered if I want a better marriage, I have to serve my wife. I also understand that I have to serve other people. If I want a better job, I start by serving my employees; I serve the people I work for; I serve my customers. I find myself waiting on the Lord. Why? Because my job is to find out what burden and yoke they have, introduce the burden to the Word of God, see if we can agree, and move on to something else. I have found that an amazing thing happens when I praise God, have the Word of God and the Holy Spirit, and spend my life in service. My confidence in God grows on a daily basis, and guess what I have? Joy!

Joy comes through my choice to love God and love what He loves. Joy comes when I have thanksgiving and praise. I have his Word. I have the Holy Spirit, and I have the opportunity to serve. That brings joy.

Your purpose on this planet is to have fun. It is for you to be filled with joy in the midst of the world's Fallen-ness. But there is a process by which the joy will enter your life. If you don't have joy in your life, start with this:

> Lord, it's not possible for me to take care of it. I can do nothing of myself. Number two, You alone are God. I'm going to let You be God. I love You. I'm going to choose to fall in love with everything You love whether I like it or not, and I'm going to follow Your Word, but I'm going to spend every day full of praise and service.

We are not striving to be happy. Happiness is a lie. Joy is not a lie. Joy is confidence in God and God's ability to do what he says. It's an astounding thing when you develop that confidence through praise, study of the Word, the Holy

Spirit, and faithful service. You have a true peace that everything is going to be fine—nothing missing, nothing broken. Your joy is the result of light and order in an otherwise dark and chaotic world. "Our Father...Hallowed by Thy name. . . Thy Kingdom come, Thy Will be done on earth, as it is in heaven" (Matthew 6:9-10, KJV). This is what our Father asks each of us to obediently do for our joy and His, and the good of all.

> The Kingdom of God is not about eating and drinking. When God reigns, the order of the day is redeeming justice, true peace, and joy made possible by the Holy Spirit.
> (Romans 14:17, VOICE).

So, first and most importantly, seek and aim at both the Kingdom and Character of God. Seek to be like the King who is full of Grace, Faith in The Truth, Love, Righteousness, Justice, and Shalom (wholeness, peace, joy, blessed):

> But first and most importantly seek [aim at, strive after] His Kingdom and His righteousness [His way of doing and being right—the attitude and character of God], and all these things will be given to you also.
> (Matthew 6:33, AMP)

By the way, "All-these-things" includes JOY!

QUESTIONS

1. Define "joy." Explain how it is developed.

2. Under what circumstances should you praise God? Why?

3. After putting your confidence in the character of God and His promises and regularly praising Him, what will occur? Why is that so important?

4. Read John 15:1-11. Meditate on the passage, and then describe the "joy" process.

K2 SERIES

CONTACT INFORMATION

Email address: K2@k2series.com

Website: www.K2series.com

Follow us on Facebook: K2series

Purchase the *K2 SERIES* of books:

Available in paperback through our website and on Amazon or as an e-book through Kindle.

Reviews appreciated.

Made in the USA
Columbia, SC
12 September 2017